A SHELTER IN THE FURY

For Steve -

Micah Exegesis Class

WCBS, Spring 1989

Ronald B. Allen

Zeph. 3:17

RONALD B. ALLEN

A SHELTER IN THE FURY

A PROPHET'S STUNNING PICTURE OF GOD

MULTNOMAH · PRESS

Portland, Oregon 97266

Old Testament quotations in this book, except where otherwise in-
dicated, are the author's personal translation.

New Testament quotations, as well as Old Testament quotations
marked (NIV), are from The Holy Bible: New International Version, © 1973, 1978, 1984 by the International Bible Society, and
used by permission of Zondervan Bible Publishers.

Scripture quotations marked (NKJV) are from The New King
James Bible, © 1984 by Thomas Nelson, Inc.

Cover design and illustration by Larry Ulmer
Edited by Steve Halliday

A SHELTER IN THE FURY
© 1986 by Multnomah Press
Portland, Oregon 97266

Multnomah Press is a ministry of Multnomah School of the Bible.

Printed in the United States of America

Library of Congress Cataloging-in-Publication Data

Allen, Ronald Barclay.
 A shelter in the fury.

 1. Bible. OT. Zephaniah—Criticism, interpretation, etc.
I. Title.
BS1645.2.A45   1986   224'.9606   86-18229
ISBN 0-88070-158-7

86 87 88 89 90 91 – 10 9 8 7 6 5 4 3 2 1

In memory of

Timothy Burg
(28 March 1983—4 March 1986)

In your brief life
We have been brought near
the Hiding Place
of our Savior.

In your new life
You are sheltered
in his very arms!

CONTENTS

INTRODUCTION

> It may be that you will be hidden
> In the day of the LORD's anger . . .
> He will quiet you with his love,
> He will rejoice over you with singing.
>   (Zephaniah 2:3, 3:17 NKJV)

What amazing words these are!
    They speak of God's awesome anger.
        They speak of God's tender love.
           They suggest his joyful song.

There is no more fearful a concept than the wrath of God.

There is no more tender a notion than the love of God.

There is no more satisfying an idea than the thought of being sheltered securely in the enveloping power of a caring God in the midst of a time of overwhelming trouble.

These are major ideas of biblical revelation.

These are particularly the ideas of the little book of Zephaniah, one of the Minor Prophets in the Hebrew Scriptures.

The small, neglected book of Zephaniah presents these ideas in balance. Here we learn how these concepts relate to each other.

More than that, in this little book we learn how we may avert God's anger and live in his love—today, tomorrow and forever.

INTRODUCTION

In the process we discover the book of Zephaniah is a door to the Hebrew prophets, a key to understanding major issues in biblical theology, and a practical guide to living the life of faith in a faithless day, and finding a sure place of hope in a hopeless day.

We have heard of the wrath of God, and we shudder with fear before him.

We have heard of the love of God, and we wistfully warm to him, desiring to know him better.

We have hoped for the sheltering song of God, and have wondered how we might find and enjoy that song.

Here it is. These are all in the book of Zephaniah. It is here that we learn to hear his song and feel his love, even as we observe his wrath.

This is not a theology of convenience or of one's own devising. This is the theology of the Bible. It is God's truth about himself. It is presented here with a sincere desire to encourage you to commit yourself to the Lord more fully than ever. As the days grow more perilous, making that commitment is more needful than ever.

PART ONE

Discovering
the
Hiding Place

CHAPTER
1

In the
Day Before

Not long ago one of the largest audiences in the history of television watched a dramatization of what might happen if the unthinkable were to take place. What would happen to the pitiable survivors of a nuclear holocaust? The drama, "The Day After" was given enormous publicity before its showing. Critical responses were mixed, as might be expected for a subject of such inherent controversy.

Criticisms of artistic merit versus political agendas aside, two scenes from that dramatization are etched deeply in my memory.

First, I think of the scene in which the missiles were unleashed. I remember the sinking feeling within as I watched the silos open in their peaceful, rural environments, and then saw the warhead-laden missiles surge and soar into the sky. There was a sense of inevitable doom in that scene. There was no help. There was no changing of the mind. There was only a pervasive sense of horror.

The second memorable scene occurred at the end. The central figure, played by Jason Robards, slumped before the rubble of his home. Then he reached out to another pitiable creature. They held each other in a parody of comfort, for there was no hope for either of them. Both were doomed, as were all others in that scene.

Firm Foundation

Music buttressed the scene in unintentional irony. The composer had selected an early American melody from the great hymn, "How Firm a Foundation." Published reports tell us that the composer at the time was unaware of the supreme irony in his choice of music.

The film took no thought of a firm foundation. It took little thought of God. It had only thoughts of doom and distress, and an appeal for the abandonment of nuclear arms before we find our world destroyed by them.

The film underscored the ultimate horrors that are inescapable in our thinking in the waning days of the second millennium A.D. The very abbreviation "A.D." seems to mock us here. *Anno Domini*. The Year of Our Lord. It seems to be anything but a year of the presence, power, and love of God.

It also seems that the last thing people really believe in these days is a hiding place in God. In fact, it is hard to know what people really believe about God at all.

Despite polls claiming that a high percentage of Americans profess belief in God, most people generally give little thought to him. The word "God" is a serviceable expletive, a filler in oaths, a little word in a busy life. But few give real thought to the person of God. To his nature. To his reality. To coming judgment. To deliverance.

A Strange Little Word

What about you? What are your thoughts of God? When you do think of God, what are the images that come to mind?

- Do you think of a kindly grandfather, unfairly doting on his favorites from some cloudy expanse way up above? Such a god might be all right if one could stay on his good side. If not, watch out!

- Perhaps you think of God as a superfigure who defies the grave and petty things that so limit us, who is above the mortal issues of illness and dying, of hurting and crying. Such a god is little help for us in our hurts; the very fact of his imperviousness further grinds us down.
- Your view of God may not be positive at all. You may be angry at God, unforgiving of what you believe to be his assaults upon your life and happiness. Perhaps you have concluded, as one well-publicized rabbi has, that God is not able to control the evil in the universe, and is not to be held responsible for the misfortune that comes into our lives. In any event, a capricious deity is no call for praise. A limited deity leaves us objects of pity.
- God, for you, may be a spoiler of fun, a divine kill-joy, who gets his own pleasure by bringing you trouble. This god is ghoulish, malevolent, angry, nasty. He is to be feared, not in reverence, but in terror.
- Your god may be a patsy. Perhaps you view God as a pushover. You may lie to him, cajole him, trick him, manipulate him. In the end, the power is in your pocket, not his.
- Perhaps for you the thought of God is an irrelevance. God was a necessary construct in simpler, more primitive days. But in our modern, technological world, one simply does not need a view of God, adequate or not.

Whatever your thoughts of God, it is not likely when you groped for a response that your mind jumped to the book of Zephaniah. Not likely at all!

A Strange Little Book

Zephaniah!

The name doesn't elicit much response these days. At most, a shrug.

"Zephaniah?"

The very sound seems quaint, old fashioned. The name, perhaps, of an early frontiersman from Tennessee: Zephaniah Randolf Smith. What a fine sobriquet for a man armed with a muzzle-loader, blending into the woods to face bears and unknown nasties.

"Zephaniah in the Bible."

Oh, *that* Zephaniah.

One of the kings? "Hezekiah, Josiah, Zephaniah?"

One of the books? "Jeremiah, Zechariah, Zephaniah?"

That's it. One of the books. One of the books in the clean, unmarked part of the Bible. One of the prophets. But one of the *Minor* Prophets. It's there all right, but not too important.

Moderns don't bother much with the little book of Zephaniah. (Moderns hardly give thought to the great book of Isaiah!)

Oh, Zephaniah is part of the Bible, all right. But it's not one of the books we read. It's one of the books we believe in; it's just not one of the ones we care about.

Zephaniah

Zephaniah for the modern reader? Only a dedicated Hebrew teacher could think of this one! Zephaniah? Would even a rabbi feel his pulse quicken at the name?

May one write a Christian book centering on Zephaniah?

Perhaps.

And then let him make a go of a sushi bar in Fargo. *Zephaniah*!

One of God's prophets.

One of the books of the Bible.

A part of the revelation of Yahweh.

Zephaniah is a treasure lost in the back pages of the Bible, sunk like a Spanish galleon off the Florida coast.

16

Here is a book lying in deep, murky waters, waiting for the bold and daring to dive down to it and seize its splendors.

The very neglect of the book becomes its strength. There is nothing like the beauty of an old treasure rediscovered by a new people.

The book of Zephaniah may speak to you in the power of the Spirit of God—even as it spoke to Hebrew people thousands of years ago.

Zephaniah is more than an exotic book lost in the sea of the Hebrew Scriptures. It is a treasure that speaks of the wonder of knowing God in tumultuous days—days like our own.

Zephaniah lived in a time of national despair and international disaster. In such a time he found solitude and peace in knowing God.

- He found a hiding place—in the shadow of Shaddai.
- He heard a song—the song of his Savior.

As you read this book, you will gain Zephaniah's secret. Next time you hear the word "Zephaniah," it will no longer evoke a shrug, but a song.

So let's make the jump together. There's a treasure that's ours. We're nearly alone in these waters. And the treasure is the shelter of the Savior, the singing of the Lord.

Later for the sushi. Let's go on to the book!

Here we will learn to think of God as he reveals himself to us. Here we will learn to think rightly about ourselves. Here we will find a way to live in the day before the day after.

CHAPTER
2

Hidden
in the Lord

Names have meaning in the Bible, meaning that aids our understanding of the story line. Names in biblical times were taken from nouns and verbs in common use—much different from names in our day.

Our names have such varied histories from so many national and ethnic stocks, that only an expert— or expectant parents with a book on names—can find the meaning. Some of us do not even know the meaning of our own names.

People in ancient Israel, as in many closed ethnic communities that may be found even today, knew the meanings of the names they used for themselves and their children and friends. Names were no mystery. They were far more than labels. They were capsules of character, ciphers of meaning, symbols of hope in God and describers of personality.

Names were regarded to *speak*.

We don't always know what the ancient names meant, of course. But when we do know the meaning of a name, it is uncanny how often the meaning parallels the direction of the person's story.

A Prophet's Name

The name *Zephaniah* is a case in point. The name of this ancient prophet is built on two Hebrew words, a verb meaning "to hide" and the proper name of God, Yahweh. *Zephaniah* means "Hidden by Yahweh."

The name was given to the prophet by his parents. But its selection was providential. Not only did it express the faith of the parents as they named their little child with this declaration of God's protective care. This name also became the signal for our interpretation of the major significance of the prophet's life and message.

God worked through the naming of this prophet as surely as he worked in the angelic announcement of the name of the Savior Jesus.

Hidden by Yahweh. This was the prophet's name. In these words we have captured one of the finest aspects of the revelation of God's grace in the Bible. For all his wrath, with all his power, in all his grand majesty—the God of Scripture delights in being known as a hiding place for his people.

As we reflect on the name of the prophet Zephaniah, we realize that this name is no aberration. It is in fact a part of the ongoing revelation of God that began with the fathers and mothers of Israel. The name Zephaniah is a further development of the old name for God in the Hebrew Bible, *El Shaddai.*

A Name for God

A Hiding Place in God. This seems to be the essential meaning of the mysterious older name for God, *Shaddai.* The enormous popularity of the contemporary Christian song "El Shaddai" has brought this name of God into new prominence among many people. Though the song is well-known, people continue to ask, What does the name "El Shaddai" mean?

Not long ago I had a special opportunity to interact with the composer of this song, John Thompson. John and his wife Patti were working on a full-scale musical based on "El Shaddai." I spent a weekend with them in Nashville and we explored together the biblical usage of this important, but debated word.

Together we rediscovered Psalm 91:1-2, a principal source for understanding the meaning of "Shaddai" and of coming to grips with the notion of being hidden by the Lord.

As I think of the book of Zephaniah and of the meaning of his name, I find myself drawn back to Psalm 91 as a source for our understanding of the underlying themes of the book.

A Poet Sings of Shaddai

Here are the opening words of Psalm 91 (NIV):

> He who dwells in the shelter of the Most High
> will rest in the shadow of the Almighty.
> I will say of the LORD, "He is my refuge and
> my fortress,
> my God, in whom I trust."

The word translated *Almighty* is the Hebrew term *shaddai*. The phrasing of the verse is even more lovely in this way: "He rests in the shadow of Shaddai."

Some once argued that the meaning of *shaddai* was related to the Hebrew word for "breast." Then they reasoned that the word would speak of God as a source of nourishment for his people. The word *shaddai* was thought to mean "The Provider."

Today we believe the meaning of *shaddai* is more likely related to an Akkadian word for "mountain." Akkadian is a Semitic language (related to biblical Hebrew), spoken by the peoples of ancient Babylon and Assyria.

When we hear the word *Shaddai* we should think of a mountain, and the associations that a mountain brings to mind.

We who live in the Pacific Northwest have no difficulty thinking of mountain grandeur. The splendid peaks of the Cascades are dramatically individual, wonderfully present. Mount Baker, Mount Rainier, Mount Adams, Mount Hood, Mount St. Helens, Mount Jefferson, The Three Sisters—each of these peaks stands as a monument of greatness.

A great pinnacle speaks majesty.
  A great peak portends durability.
    A great mountain suggests prominence.
    Wonder.
      Stability.
        Grandeur.
         God!

A mountain becomes a strong image for God. Moses was drawn to speaking of God as "the Rock" (in Deuteronomy 32, see verses 4, 15, 18, 30, 31). So was David, who wrote, "Praise be to Yahweh my Rock" (Psalm 144:1), and "Yahweh is my rock, my fortress and my deliverer" (Psalm 18:2).

Mountain Majesty

It was often in the context of mountains that God displayed his wonder. Think of Moses hidden on Mount Sinai in the cleft of the rock when the glory of God passed by (Exodus 33:22).

Similarly, Elijah waited on the revelation of the glory of God while hidden in the cave of Mount Horeb (1 Kings 19:9). Perhaps these two great prophets were hiding in the very same place, since Horeb is another name for Sinai. The definite article in the Hebrew text in 1 Kings 19:9 [*"the* cave"] suggests a cave previously known by the reader. Such a cave was the cleft in the rock used by Moses, whose spirit Elijah was attempting to recapture in this dramatic, touching story.

The poet of Psalm 91 builds on these themes. These are his words again, in a personal translation:

> One who dwells in the shelter of Elyon
>   resides in the shadow of Shaddai.
> I say of Yahweh, "My refuge, my mountain
>   stronghold",
>   of my God, "I trust in him."

There are several designations for God used in this passage. In addition to the regularly recurring words

God (Hebrew, *'elohim*) and the principal divine name *Yahweh* (conventionally rendered "LORD"), this text also pairs the rarer words *Elyon* (the Most High) and *Shaddai* (the Almighty).

The Highest

The word *Elyon* fits so nicely here with the word *Shaddai*. If we are correct in our understanding that Shaddai speaks of God in the imagery of a majestic mountain, then the balancing term "Most High" is a most apt choice.

The psalm speaks of the Lord as a high, lofty, secure mountain fortress. Those who have visited the land of Israel will have their thoughts drawn to the impressive site Masada, on the western bank of the Dead Sea. On that lofty, high, isolated promontory the ancients could imagine withstanding all foes for an indefinite period of time, if only their provisions would be sufficient.

The Fortress

It was at Masada that the paranoid King Herod had a magnificent retreat palace constructed, thinking he could flee there if things went against him in Judah. He supplied the storerooms and the cisterns with sufficient food and water, wine and oil, to last a proverbial thousand men a hundred years.

As it was, Herod did not flee to this site. Fugitive zealots from the Roman war against Judea came here for their last stand. The story of their last days is an appalling cross between the Alamo and Jonestown.

Masada was a place of last-ditch defense against overwhelming odds. It was also the place of dreadful tragedy. When the Jewish people saw their doom take inevitable shape in the form of a nearly complete Roman assault ramp, they decided to commit suicide—a most uncharacteristic Jewish action! For them, dying as free men and women was preferable to defeat and to slavery and abuse under the Roman fist.

Masada is a symbol in reverse. Israeli paratroopers now take their oath of allegiance to the state, shouting the stirring words: "Never again!" Never again will Jewish people be brought to such a point of stress that suicide seems the only way out.

But the mount stands. It stands today as it has through time. It stands today as it did in the time of David. He came here in one period in his flight from Saul. He could not linger, as the only provisions he had were those he and his men had carried. But while on that high fortress he had the sense of invincibility. The mount is so high, the sides so steep, the view so clear round about—here is shelter indeed.

The Sheltering Place

So the images of Psalm 91 come together.

- the shelter of Elyon
- the shadow of Shaddai
- my refuge
- my mountain stronghold

I am so drawn to the phrase, *the shadow of Shaddai*. The imagery of this verse suggests an oppressively hot region in Judah and a traveler alone in a hostile land.

With the sun burning down and with enemies moving about, all at once the harried believer finds a cleft in the rocky face of his hostile environment.

He moves into the cleft and at once finds shelter. Of a sudden he enjoys shade. In a moment he discovers protection.

It's like coming home to God.

So the psalmist shouts:

> I say of Yahweh:
> "My refuge! My mountain fortress!"
> of my God,
> "I trust in him!"
> (Psalm 91:2)

Several years ago our family spent a summer in Israel with a group of seminary students. Our group spent one long, hot day hiking in the Wilderness of Zin in southern Judah. The heat was relentless. The terrain was rugged and barren. Rock and sand were the only sights below. The sun was the supreme reality above.

Dr. James Fleming, our guide for the day, had us round a bend at the scheduled time for lunch. All at once we came upon a cleft in the rock. We climbed up . . . and entered a new world.

Water could be heard moving in the inner recesses of the cleft. At once we were cool. We were sheltered. We were safe from sun and storm. We had discovered the meaning of finding a hiding place in the rock.

I then read the words of Psalm 91 to our student group. These were not just words we read and heard. They were words that had become a part of our experience. With the psalmist we imaged God as a magnificent mountain who graciously provided for us a cleft to hide from the assaults of life. Our simple bagged lunch seemed to taste better that day than on any other. Even the hard boiled eggs tasted good!

We had come to a resting spot that was a picture from an Old Testament poem. It was splendid!

The prophet Zephaniah was named for such an experience. His message was designed for others to evoke this image of finding a resting place in God.

There are two images in Psalm 91 that describe a resting place in God. One is the high, powerful mountain with the cleft for the person of faith. The second is more maternal.

A Mother Hen

This second image is the familiar biblical picture of a chick seeking refuge under the wings of the mother hen. This, too, is a part of the biblical portrait of the Father.

- He is towering mountain.
- He is sheltering hen.

Here are the words of the psalm:

Surely he will save you from the fowler's snare
and from the deadly pestilence.
He will cover you with his feathers,
and under his wings you will find refuge;
his faithfulness will be your shield and rampart.
(Psalm 91:3-4 NIV)

Those of us who live in urban areas have limited opportunities to experience the animal imagery of the Bible up close. Goats, sheep and chickens, so much a part of the biblical world, are a very small part of ours.

One of the impractical, romantic ideas in the back of my mind some years ago was to move to the country where I could learn something about the animals that so frequently move across the story line of the biblical pages.

One discovery our family has made since making such a move concerns the image of the mother hen and her brood of chicks. There is simply nothing I know to compare with the flight of little chicks to the enveloping wings of their mother.

We once witnessed this dramatically. A hen we believed to have "flown the coop" showed up on the front lawn one day with thirteen baby chicks following her single file. It was right out of a Disney cartoon.

There she was, strutting her stuff. And behind her came her brood, each chick stumbling after the other in a drawn-out line.

That night we put the hen with the chickens and the chicks in a box under a light. The next day we cleaned out the brooding area with care. We put down fresh litter. We put the chicks in their new home. Then we went for the mother.

Have you ever tried to ask one chicken in a flock if she is the mother? We didn't know which was the right one!

We put one hen in with the chicks. Nothing happened.

Then we put in the next hen. Again, nothing. Just some scratching in the litter.

Then the third.

It happened so fast, we nearly missed it. She swooped with her wings and the chicks disappeared. All thirteen of them. They were completely hidden. She seemed then to be especially wary, daring someone to touch her chicks again.

God is like that mother hen. When he stretches out his wings and his people come near, they are protected and comforted. They are sheltered and cared for in an embrace of love.

The hen will last. Her protection is sure.

The psalmist knew this so well. He wrote:

> For he delivers you
>> from the fowler's snare,
>> from destructive pestilence;
> by his wing, he protectively covers you,
>> and under his wings you may seek refuge;
>> his faithfulness is a solid shield.
>>>> (Psalm 91:3-4)

Faithfulness as Shield

Just how the last phrasing, "his faithfulness is a solid shield," relates to the imagery of the mother hen may be perplexing. How faithful is a hen? How solid her shield?

The late Dr. J. Edwin Hartill, a long-time pastor in Minnesota, visited a farmer on a tragic day.

The farmer's barn had burned down. Hay had been brought in too wet. Fire began spontaneously. The farmer's spirit was broken.

Together farmer and pastor walked out to the remains of the barn. Most of the smoking timbers had been pulled clear of the cement foundation. As they walked along, the farmer saw a smoking thing just before him.

"Oh, no," he grimaced. "Even the barn hen is dead!"

He gave the smoking hulk a kick with his boot, an act of anger and frustration.

No sooner had he kicked the dead hen than he and the pastor were startled to see three little chicks running around in a circle where the hen had been.

That hen, in demonstration of love for her chicks, had literally roasted to death to keep them alive.

The ancients knew how hens cared for their young. They knew what it was for chicks to run for refuge to seek the comforting wings of their mother.

They also knew what it was to come to the sheltering care of God. They imaged God as protecting hen.

Centuries later, our Lord would look out with distress over the city of Jerusalem, a city which had rejected his message and spurned his salvation. He would then apply to himself the tender, loving picture of God as mother hen:

> O Jerusalem, Jerusalem . . . how often I have longed to gather your children together, as a hen gathers her chicks under her wings, but you were not willing! (Luke 13:34)

These words of Jesus did not innovate a new level of God's concern for the welfare of his people. Jesus was expressing the desire that has always been a part of the loving heart of God. It is just that, in Jesus, the words sound even stronger because we hear them from his mouth directly.

This is the message of the prophets and the poets of the Hebrew Bible. It is the message of Zephaniah, encapsuled in his name: *Hidden by Yahweh*.

So We Learn God

The word "God" was not a little word to the people of faith in biblical times. *God* is the supreme reality for a person of faith. God is not grandfather nor bionic superperson. God is not patsy nor impotent.

For people of faith throughout time, God is *Lord*.

For people of faith, God is *refuge*.

For people of faith, Yahweh is *Shaddai*—the hiding place secure and sound.

28

These were the discoveries of the psalmists. They were also the hope of the prophets. God as Hiding Place is a principal presentation of the great minor prophet Zephaniah.

But these realities are not "automatic." They are conditional—conditioned upon our response to Yahweh. J. Richard Chase, president of Wheaton College, emphasizes the conditional nature of the promises of Psalm 91:

> Psalm 91 cannot be "trotted out" when Satan is pursuing us and we are away from everybody and want to kick over the traces. This Psalm cannot be "trotted out" when somehow or other we are caught in a situation where pride moves us in a wrong direction. This Psalm is for those who dwell "in the secret place of the most High." If we do that, God has assured us that Satan cannot enter in and cause us to besmirch the Lord Jesus Christ by our actions.[1]

We should not be surprised to find these concepts in the great little book of the prophet Zephaniah. After all, this was the meaning of his name.

Now it's time to hear some of his words.

---

1. J. Richard Chase, "Don't Just Visit the Secret Place of the Most High—Live There!" *Decision,* February, 1986, p. 14.

PART TWO

Facing
Judgment

C H A P T E R
3

A Clean
Sweep

An immensely popular Christian pastor in southern California directs his distinctive ministry to people who need encouragement—and who doesn't? This high-voltage parson in the electronic church makes much of the positive concept of possibility instead of negative ideas of defeat and discouragement. Robert Schuller has identified the Christian faith with what he calls "possibility thinking," an advanced hybrid of the positive thinking of his mentor, Dr. Norman Vincent Peale.

Schuller even has his own Bible. He has prepared an edition of the Bible in which verses that lead to "possibility thinking" are highlighted in blue. A reader can open this Bible to nearly any page and find verses that will inspire positive attitudes.

The opening words of the prophet Zephaniah are *not* highlighted in Schuller's Bible! The reason is not hard to discover. Here is how Zephaniah's message begins:

> [Yahweh speaking]
> "I will sweep away everything
> from the face of the earth,"
>   declares Yahweh.
>   (Zephaniah 1:2 NIV,
>   with "Yahweh" substituted for "the
>   LORD," and so throughout this book)

Gasp! Little room for "possibility thinking" here.

Schuller and Scripture

Saying Schuller has his critics is akin to observing there are numerous cars in Los Angeles. Some are quite harsh in taking Schuller to task. They charge him with minimizing the Bible, with trivializing the gospel, with a style-over-substance showmanship.

Each is a serious charge.

Each may be overstated.

Schuller responds to his critics by saying that his approach *works*. He argues that people misrepresent his approach as just a self-serving means of gratification. He says possibility thinking is simply the secular term for faith. He points to numerous people who have responded to his ministry when they would not have listened to more traditional approaches. He tells of many who have turned to hope in God in the midst of desperate distress. He also says that his ministry is not to be judged against the same standards used to evaluate traditional church congregations. His ministry is directed to the unchurched, and should be evaluated in that light.

Prophets and Possibilities

Whatever we may think of the approach used by the Reverend Dr. Schuller, one thing is certain. His positive-attitude approach to sinners is a world away from the approach of the Old Testament prophets.

Zephaniah, Jeremiah, and Isaiah did not center on what Schuller calls "possibility thinking."

But this is not just a contrast with Dr. Schuller. To imply that it is would be a cheap shot! It would be hard to imagine *anyone* today having precisely the same approach the prophets used during the Old Testament period.

If the direct, harsh, and frontal methods of the prophets are designed to be the strict standards for Christian ministry today, not only would Robert

Schuller be faulted. So, to some degree, would be Billy Graham, Jerry Falwell, Bill Bright, Earl Radmacher, John MacArthur, Charles Swindoll, Pat Robertson, J. Vernon McGee, or nearly anyone else (including myself!).

The prophets begin so negatively that we hardly know how to relate to them today. Even Billy Sunday must have smiled before he took off his coat and began to wrestle the devil.

"Nice" and the Bible

To put it bluntly, *the prophets were not nice.*

As much as we use it, *nice* is a weak word. It's not really a biblical term, nor a biblical concept.

But *nice* seems to be an important word in our culture. We're naturally drawn to "nice" people, repelled by the not-nice. Sometimes a person who is right, but who is not nice, will lose a hearing because of a caustic attitude.

How shall we learn to listen to the prophets who are not nice? For they really are not.

Zephaniah does not even begin by saying how glad he is for the opportunity to speak to us. *Every* speaker at least begins with words of appreciation for such opportunities.

Zephaniah begins with words of such stunning judgment we reel before them. He walks up, swings his fist in the solar plexus, then hits again before we've caught our breath. It's the Rambo approach to prophecy.

Here again are his opening words, this time in a personal translation, as will be many other Old Testament quotations in this book:

> "I will most certainly sweep away everything
> from the face of the earth"
>   —solemn utterance of Yahweh!
> "I will sweep away man and beast,
> I will sweep away birds of the heavens
> and fish of the sea.

> I will thrust aside the wicked,
>   and I will cut off man
>   from the face of the earth"
>   —solemn utterance of Yahweh!
>   (Zephaniah 1:2-3)

Give Us Jesus

No wonder people do not know much about the prophets. No wonder people don't like the Old Testament. No wonder people turn to the Schullers of this age. Much better to have the "Be-Happy Attitudes" than the pessimism of this type of text.

"Give us Jesus. At least he is nice."

Jesus speaks to people with dignity. Jesus holds little children in his arms. Jesus offers hope. Jesus is the Shepherd!

"Give us Jesus. Leave the old prophets lie."

And yet . . .

Is Jesus "Nice"?

Is it really true that Jesus is always "nice"?

Does a "nice" man speak to people the way Jesus did from time to time? We seem to remember his comforting words more easily than his condemnatory words.

The same person who offers the sweet blessings of a caring God to the poor, the weak and the disenfranchised in the Beatitudes (Matthew 5:3-12), also speaks in the following way to people who ignored his words and works and did not repent of their sin:

> Woe to you, Korazin! Woe to you, Bethsaida! If the miracles that were performed in you had been performed in Tyre and Sidon, they would have repented long ago in sackcloth and ashes. But I tell you, it will be more bearable for Tyre and Sidon on the day of judgment than for you.
>
> And you, Capernaum, will you be lifted up to the skies? No, you will go down to the depths. If the miracles that were performed in

you had been performed in Sodom, it would have remained to this day. But I tell you that it will be more bearable for Sodom on the day of judgment than for you. (Matthew 11:21-24)

Surprised? Well, hold on.

Here are words he had for religious authorities who opposed the truth he presented:

Woe to you, teachers of the law and Pharisees, you hypocrites! You build tombs for the prophets and decorate the graves of the righteous. And you say, "If we had lived in the days of our forefathers, we would not have taken part with them in shedding the blood of the prophets." So you testify against yourselves that you are the descendants of those who murdered the prophets. Fill up, then, the measures of the sin of your forefathers!

You snakes! You brood of vipers! How will you escape being condemned to hell? (Matthew 23:29-33)

Gasp! The same sweet Jesus who comforted grieving parents, who fed the hungry, who raised the dead, also was the Jesus who spoke prophetically of judgment scenes as vividly as any Old Testament prophet.

Jesus' apocalyptic Sermon on the Mount of Olives (Matthew 24-25) is not nearly so well known as his comforting Sermon on the Mount (Matthew 5-7). The phrasings of this impassioned, condemnatory message breathe the same spirit as the prophets of old. In fact, it is only with a deep acquaintance with the messages of the Old Testament prophets that the imagery of the Savior in these chapters may be understood.

Faithfulness and Kindness

Here is the point. Zephaniah was not "nice." But then, neither was Jesus. Jesus was kind—when kindness served people the best. But Jesus could use words as a scirocco wind, blasting with heat and smarting with intensity beyond expectation.

Please don't get me wrong. I like to be around nice, pleasant people. And I usually desire to be nice myself. Yet there are times when being "nice" is doing no favor at all. If one were suffering from a malignancy that needed immediate treatment, a doctor might be "nice" in hiding the trouble, but the physician would not be kind at all if she did not tell the patient the worst and then begin working toward the best.

In fact, the most unkind thing of all would have been for Zephaniah or Jesus to have been "nice" in the face of God's impending judgment. It is no kindness to say, "Peace, peace" to a people who are at war. It is not pleasantness to say, "Have a nice day!" to a person who is entering a theater you know to be on fire. A lot what goes for "nice," may not really be nice at all.

Zephaniah and Jesus were not "nice." But they *were* both faithful. They were faithful to the word of Yahweh they had been given. They were commanded to tell people the worst first. Only then could plans be made for the best.

Possibility thinking is not all wrong. But before the possibilities can be explored, the worst-case scenario has to be made known. It is a kindness in the last resort.

Glory to God

At the end of Jesus' ministry, he was able to look back on the years of public presentation of God's word and say to his Father: "I have brought you glory on earth by completing the work you gave me to do" (John 17:4).

The work of Jesus in bringing the glory of God to earth included both words of kindness to poor and hurting people *and* words of judgment to unrepentant sinners.

In the same manner (but to a lesser degree), the prophet Zephaniah was able to come to the end of his days and affirm that he had completed the task on earth God gave him to do. What God gave Zephaniah to do was much more than to present "Be-Happy Attitudes." He had come to present the fullness of the word of God for a desperately needy day. He came with harshness and judgment. He also came with mercy and hope. The balanced ministry of the word of God does both.

Only in this balance could true glory be given to God on earth by his servants the prophets and by his Son the Savior.

Exploring the Possibilities

Here, in my view, is the difficulty with the popular, consciously positive ministries of men such as Robert Schuller and Norman Vincent Peale. These positive-oriented ministries may be genuinely helpful to some people, but merely a poultice on a malignancy to others.

A Christian can read these books, listen to their messages, and be much impressed with the need for a more positive, cheerful attitude in facing the stresses of life. This is most helpful indeed. Many Christians need to develop a "possibility thinker's" approach and "be-happy" attitudes. The church has too many people whose hope-quotient has rotted to the core. These have lost the joy of the Lord and they do not really know his power to overcome troubles through them. The down attitudes of many Christian people seem prompted not by piety so much as by spiritual indigestion. If Schuller can give them spiritual Rolaids, so much the better for all of us. Some need relief, no matter how it is spelled.

But what about the nonbeliever? What about the person who has not come to faith in Christ, but who finds the writings of Schuller to be helpful in meeting needs of attitude change and personal growth? When this person stops there, he or she may be a happier person, but is no better suited for eternity. What will come of "possibility thinking" when the unregenerate faces the wrath of an angry God? It will not help to have a happy face if one has not faced soundly the ultimate consequences of sin.

It is here that we may contrast the self-consciously positive ministry of Schuller and the more balanced ministries of those we have mentioned earlier. None of us wishes to begin as does Zephaniah. But none of us dare ignore his warnings either. Our style may be different than the prophet's, but our message had better include what he says!

The Lord's Broom

Zephaniah was commissioned by God to prepare a faithful minority for days of terrible distress in the coming wrath of God against unrepentant sinners. This was more than "possibility thinking." When it comes down to it, he presents *the only real thinking possible*. The opening words of Zephaniah present the imagery of a God about to sweep away all things in solemn judgment.

Picture God standing on a back porch strewn with leaves blown in from fall winds. Broom in hand, he begins to sweep away the piles of leaves.

Closer up, we see it is not leaves he is about to sweep.

It is people!

Sinning people litter his porch; he is about to sweep them from the deck of his presence. Here is the Creator about to destroy his creation, the maker undoing his work.

As a computer screen might cause all words to disappear at a keyed command, so the creation is about to vanish from the screen of God's presence.

I do my writing on a personal computer. My wife Beverly is now learning to use the computer in her own writing. A few days ago she spent more than ten hours working on a project. I had warned her about the necessity of being careful so as not to destroy her work. She was very careful. Things went well. Then she asked me to read her work before she printed it. And at that point I did what I had cautioned her not to do. I pressed the wrong key, and what I meant to save, I destroyed. Everything was lost, including the back-up files. Everything! Bless her heart, she whispered, "Good night," and went to bed. I suspect my action might be construed as grounds for divorce in the new computer age.

Now imagine the Creator pressing the "do not save" command, and the screen of his computer going suddenly blank. This modern update of the imagery of Zephaniah heightens the issue: God is about to destroy all that he has made.

The words of the opening oracle of God through the prophet Zephaniah speak of a *bouleversement,* a complete reversal of God's creative works. This passage calls to mind the ordered works of divine power that Genesis 1 describes. Now all is to disappear: man, beast, birds, fish. It is an unraveling of the delicately embroidered fabric of his works. It is a coming apart of his order.

It is a clean sweep.

Chilling urgency pervades these words. God has done this before! Remember the story of the Great Flood? A part of the divine purpose of that story is to remind us all that the creation remains under curse and that God's coming judgment is sure. It was water once. Next time, fire. Or as Zephaniah has it, next time by broom.

Let's read these words once more, thinking through the use of language the prophet makes in recounting God's words:

"I will most certainly sweep away everything
    from the face of the earth"
        —solemn utterance of Yahweh!
I will sweep away man and beast,
I will sweep away birds of the heavens
    and fish of the sea.

I will thrust aside the wicked,
    and I will cut off man
    from the face of the earth"
        —solemn utterance of Yahweh!
            (Zephaniah 1:2-3)

Urgent and Total

Several items in the original text of the opening oracle (1:2-3) emphasize the urgency of the message and the comprehensiveness of the coming judgment:

- the verb "to sweep away" (Hebrew *'āsap*) four times, with the parallel verb "to thrust aside"
- the repetition of the phrase "from the earth"
- the repetition of the phrase "solemn utterance of Yahweh"
- the use of "all things" and enumerated things
- the startling progression: all things, man, beast, birds, fish, the wicked, and man
- the suddenness of the oracle, with no introduction

The words of this passage sting even as we read them more than twenty-seven centuries after they were first spoken. But barely have we heard these words than we get the prophet's second punch.

Ready? Here it comes:

"I will stretch out my hand against Judah
    and against all who live in Jerusalem.
I will cut off from this place every remnant of Baal,
    the names of the pagan and the idolatrous priests—
those who bow down on the roofs
    to worship the starry host,
those who bow down and swear by Yahweh
    and who also swear by Molech,
those who turn back from following Yahweh
    and neither seek Yahweh nor inquire of him."
            (Zephaniah 1:4-6 NIV)

Those Words?

One factor makes these words of Zephaniah even harder to bear: It is when we realize that the words are in fact *the words of God himself.* The very first words of the book tell us the origin of the prophet's message: "The word of Yahweh that came to Zephaniah."

It is fitting that the message comes from the Lord through his prophet, for the basic meaning of the Hebrew word "prophet" (*nābî'*) means "one who speaks for another." The true prophets of the Bible never originated their messages. Their messages came from the Lord. They gave the message style, but the substance was from God. We will come back to this in a bit.

If we understand that it was in fact Yahweh who first said these words, then they become harder then ever. How is it that God would say such things? What kind of language is this? Is this rhetorical flourish, empty bombast, idle threat? Or is this to be taken more seriously than we have ever regarded language in life?

Listen to the first-person verbs again, and think of them as the words of God:

- "I will most certainly sweep away"
- "I will cause to totter"
- "I will cut off"
- "I will stretch out my hand against"

This last verb is perhaps the most difficult of all. Think of the many times in the Old Testament that God says he has stretched out his hand against the enemies of his people or that he has extended his hand to Israel in blessing. Think of the hands of Jesus stretched out even in his dying. Usually we think of the hand of God in pleasant terms, images of blessing and protection.

Now this hand is a fist.

Now this hand is clutching a broom.

Now this hand is stretched out against his own people.

He is threatening Judah.

> He is reaching out in judgment against Jerusalem.

We have to ask, *Why?*

As we read these verses again, we begin to gain insight into God's reasons for turning his hand of mercy into an instrument of wrath against his people.

The Turning of His People

It is because they have turned against him. The very people whom God had rescued from Egypt, redeemed, set apart and blessed—*they* had turned from him to embrace the worship of idols. False gods instead of true. Myths instead of reality.

Zephaniah's contemporary, the great Jeremiah, put it this way:

> My people have committed two sins:
> They have forsaken me,
>   the spring of living water,
> and have dug their own cisterns,
>   broken cisterns that cannot hold water.
>   (Jeremiah 2:13 NIV)

Imagine someone living in an arid land, so dependent upon infrequent rains for survival. Then he is given exclusive use of a spring gushing with fresh water in abundant supply. Then think of him abandoning the spring, digging cisterns to store runoff water from the infrequent rains, only to find the cisterns will not even hold brackish waters. This is precisely the sin of Judah. This is the indictment of the people of Jerusalem.

We begin to learn these things in verse 4 of Zephaniah 1 as we read of idolatrous acts of the people and their perfidy against Yahweh. Here are some of the details we pick up as we scan the verses again:

- There are still remnants of the old Baal cult—even in the holy city of Jerusalem.
- There are pagan, idolatrous priests in the city.

- There is the worship of stars and planets on the rooftops.
- There are people who swear loyalty to Yahweh and to their other gods, as though Yahweh were one choice in a spiritual smorgasbord.
- The people venerate the Moabite deity Milcom or Molech.
- The people have turned from God and have become disloyal to him.
- They no longer practice the piety they used to maintain:
    —they no longer seek after Yahweh,
    —they no longer inquire after him.

When we complete this list we learn that the Creator has turned on his creation because the creature has turned from him. The hand of Yahweh is stretched out in wrath. In his judgment, Yahweh is going to be all-inclusive. This is no longer to be spot surgery. This is radical surgery—general, not specific. The hand of God is directed not only against his people, but against even the planet itself.

Final judgment is in view. Here is a picture of the day after.

Again I think of Jason Robards in front of the rubble of his home, all hope gone. A fictional portrayal of the results of nuclear warfare cannot be more devastating than the prophetic picture Zephaniah presents in this awful passage.

Pretty hard to be a possibility thinker in such a setting!

Yet in these words, Zephaniah desires us to gain *the only real thinking that is possible*. We will begin to see what this is in the next chapter.

One thing is certain: A clean sweep is not a pleasant picture to one who may be caught by the broom.

4

Preparations for the Great Day

People have an insatiable appetite to know the newest speculation concerning the future. Each January, supermarket tabloids scream with bold headlines their peculiar inside scoop on what will take place in the coming year. Usually names of clairvoyants such as Jeane Dixon will ensure sales.

This year one of the tabloids outdid itself. The large headline reads:

"New Dead Sea Scrolls Reveal
1986 PREDICTIONS
FROM THE BIBLE"

The article, by Barbara Gilbert in the *Sun* (21 January 1986), may be one of the most preposterous ever concocted. The story purports to present the findings of a biblical scholar on "newly-authenticated Dead Sea Scrolls" which give specific predictions for the year 1986. Further misrepresentation comes in the large caps that identify this scroll's message with the Bible.

From the "Scrolls"

According to this article, a hitherto unknown Qumran text (from before the time of Christ) predicts such modern events as the deaths of President John F.

Kennedy, Robert Kennedy and Martin Luther King Jr., and the development of the current AIDS crisis!

With these "authenticating data," the reader is anxious to know what is new in the scroll. What new terrors will the year ahead bring?

Not to worry, says "scholar Gary Krinn" in this article. In 1986 there will be a landing on Earth of aliens from another galaxy. "These beings are visitors from the Lord who will come to negotiate our entrance into the Interplanetary Confederation."

Further, a healing angel will give physicians of the earth a new brilliance of knowledge so that "all disease will be removed from the face of the earth."

All of this "before the end of 1986." All according to a "Dead Sea Scroll newly-authenticated." All these are "predictions from the Bible."

I am currently teaching a seminary course on the Dead Sea Scrolls. We read this article in class today. It was difficult to return to the legitimate scroll material we were translating. The utter absurdity of the story simply takes the breath away.

Not one fact was given in the article concerning the scroll, the "scholar," or the methods of interpretation. Yet this is what the public seems to want when they think of "biblical prophecy."

A Caring Deity

There's something else people really desire—some sign from heaven that there is a God above who really does care about their lives and their needs.

This is the conclusion of a recent article in the *Montreal Gazette* reporting on a hoax that brought thousands of pilgrims to the home of Maurice Girouard in Ste.-Marthe-sur-le-Lac, Quebec, to observe a small statue of the Virgin Mary which seemed to be weeping and oozing blood.

A story by Associated Press reporter Charles Campbell describes laboratory results on the small statue. It had been coated with pork and beef fat and then layered with human blood. Under bright lights, the fat would liquefy and the "tears of blood" would form in droplets. The whole sad affair, declared the examining scientist, is "a pure and simple fraud, a hoax, an imposture and collective hysteria."

And the people? Why did more than twelve thousand people come in the course of a week and stand in lines in the middle of winter to see this bleeding, weeping statue? The article suggests it is because of "the deep yearning for any sign at all that some divinity cares about suffering humanity."

Specific, contemporary predictions and magically bleeding statues. These are the sorts of things that get the attention of people these days.

All the while the genuine predictive prophecies of the Bible and the deeply moving biblical accounts of God's care for suffering humanity are ignored.

The Real Thing

"Biblical scholar Gary Krinn" and the alleged statue hoaxer Maurice Girouard should have opened their Bibles. A superb place for them to have turned to would have been the book of Zephaniah.

Here they would have found the real thing. Here is where they would have found both genuine biblical prophecies and true accounts of God's concern for mankind.

As is customary in biblical prophecy—so different from the false thing—Zephaniah presents the really bad news first. He does not speak of intergalactic visitors or of dripping statues.

Zephaniah tells the horrible message of the coming of the Day of Yahweh.

Here is how he tells it.

Hush!

He begins with a call for people to hush:

> Be silent before the Sovereign Yahweh,
> for the day of Yahweh is near.
> (Zephaniah 1:7 NIV)

FACING JUDGMENT

The words "Be silent" are more literally the word "Hush!" This word "hush!" reminds me of a story told by the musician and novelist Eugenia Zukerman. She was describing her first images of God from childhood. She was sitting in front of her family television set, playing with her doll. The program changed and her attention was caught by the presence of a figure on the screen. She describes him this way:

> A man with streaming white hair and bushy eyebrows. A commanding presence. He stood on the podium, back to me; then, suddenly, he wheeled around, looked furious, placed a forbidding finger to his lips and hissed a loud and frightening "Shhhhh!" I was the only one in the room. He must be talking to me, I thought. I was mesmerized. This man had power. This must be God, I reasoned. And there are those who say Toscanini would have agreed.[1]

For most of us, the words "Be silent" suggest an altogether different image than the imperious Toscanini scaring the socks off a little girl.

A scene takes place in innumerable churches throughout the world on Sunday mornings. The choir begins the service with words that seem to be comforting and charming: "The LORD is in his holy temple, let all the earth keep silent before him."

The intent of these words, of course, is to call the congregation to quiet contemplation and reflective worship of God as they prepare for the service that is to follow. These words remind us of the calming line from the Psalms: "Be still and know that I am God."

There is so much noise and clatter in most of our lives that the opportunity for a time of quiet is refreshing, a salve for the spirit.

There is a problem in these comforting words, however. They are not supposed to relax us. They are designed to put our teeth on edge.

PREPARATIONS FOR THE GREAT DAY

The words are from the prophets, and they announce impending judgment. Zephaniah gives one setting of these words. The more familiar setting, so common in choral introits, is given in Habakkuk 2:20 (and another is in Isaiah 41:1). Even the call of the Psalms, "Be still and know that I am God," is an announcement of judgment (see Psalm 46:10 in context).

There *is* a place for a call to silence for contemplation and for the adoration of the Lord. No question! The writers of the Bible do call for this type of silence from time to time. Psalm 131 speaks of a believer quieting his soul as he draws near to God, as a child coming to its mother's breast.

But the call for silence from the prophets is of a different sort. It is a command to *hush* because of the horrors of the judgment to come. Here are Zephaniah's words again:

> *Hush!* before the Lord Yahweh,
>   for the day of Yahweh is near!
> For Yahweh has ordained a sacrifice,
>   he has sanctified his guests.
>   (Zephaniah 1:7)

The Hebrew verb I have translated as "Hush!" is in fact very nearly the same sound as our English word, a term known to chattering children everywhere.

But this is not hushing before an impatient parent or a busy teacher. It is a call to hush in the presence of the Master of the universe, the great Sovereign of all creation.

He is about to institute his special day. It is now very near.

The verses that follow ripple with references to time:

- "for near is the day of Yahweh" (verse 7)
- "a day of the sacrifice of Yahweh" (verse 8)

- "in that day" (verse 9)
- "and it will be in that day" (verse 10)
- "and it will be at that time" (verse 12)
- "the sound of the day of Yahweh" (verse 14)
- "a day of . . . " (six times, verses 15-16)
- "in the day of the fury of Yahweh" (verse 18)

It is difficult to emphasize too much this notion of the day of Yahweh, given these data. It is a day that is specific and terrible. It is a day known to him and which will come to pass in his time.

A second emphasis we observe in these verses concerns the nearness of the Day of Yahweh:

- "for near is the day of Yahweh" (verse 7)
- "near is the great day of Yahweh" (verse 14)
- "near and coming exceedingly soon" (also in 14)

A third aspect of the coming of this day has to do with the personal, dramatic, profound actions of Yahweh himself. This aspect is seen in the action verbs spoken of God or by him:

- "for Yahweh has established a sacrifice" (verse 7)
- "he has sanctified his guests" (verse 7)
- "I will punish—visit in wrath" (three times: verses 8, 9 and 12)
- "I will search out" (verse 12)
- "I will bring distress" (verse 17)
- "he will make a sudden end" (verse 18)

Yet a fourth factor is the wickedness of man that prompts such actions by Yahweh the compassionate. The reasons for God's anger are not given in this section at once. We wonder, as this section begins in verse 7, what it might be that has gotten the Lord so very angry. What possibly could so provoke his wrath? Further, we wonder if it is really true that God's wrath will be addressed against his own people, and especially against his holy city Jerusalem.

In verse 8 we learn that the day of sacrifice begins against the royal house of Judah:

> I will visit in wrath the princes,
>> even the sons of the king,
> and all who clothe themselves
>> with foreign clothing.
>
> (Zephaniah 1:8)

The fact that judgment begins with the royal house is nearly as unsettling as the fact it comes to the holy city. Has not Yahweh promised he will establish the throne of David and his royal house for all generations? Yet as we think through the provisions of the Davidic Covenant, which is the divine grant to the house of David for a perpetual line of kings, we remember even in this covenant the words of warning. 2 Samuel 7 provided for the chastening of the king by Yahweh should the king prove himself faithless to God's covenant.

In Zephaniah 1:7-8 the fault seems to lie upon the "foreign clothing," an aspect, perhaps, of the untoward foreign influences in the royal house of Judah.

Dress by itself would not provoke the terrible judgment this passage is about to present. It must have been more than clothing. Rather, the foreignness of the clothing and its very opulence speak of disloyalty to God.

The repeated verb of God's judgment, which the NIV translates "I will punish" (as in verse 8), is the significant term *pāqaḏ*. An extraordinarily rich word, this verb means "to miss," and then "to come to visit." The visit may be in mercy. It may also be in wrath.

In the lovely story in the book of Ruth, Naomi learned while she was still in Moab that Yahweh had *visited* his people to return to them the productivity of the land (Ruth 1:6). This is an example of Yahweh's coming to visit in mercy and blessing.

Zephaniah uses the verb in its most negative sense;

hence the NIV translates the verb in these verses as "I will punish."

In Ruth, God had come to give bread; here he comes to institute a grisly sacrifice. What a frightening use of this word!

Pagan Practices

It was not only arrogance and opulence in the royal family that was about to bring the wrath of the Lord. It was particularly the pagan practices that had come to the people and their priests, and which entered even the temple itself.

Zephaniah reports this charge of Yahweh:

> On that day I will punish
> all who avoid stepping on the threshold,
> who fill the temple of their gods
> with violence and deceit.
> (Zephaniah 1:9 NIV)

The reasons for God's wrath become clearer. As in the days of Isaiah—and as in the days of Jesus!—the people were trampling the courts of God. He will not abide the misuse of his holy place.

But here it was worse than in the days of Isaiah or of Jesus. It was not just that they worshiped Yahweh improperly. They were in fact worshiping pagan deities in the very courts established for the worship of the Lord. Here was a defilement of the temple, a polluting of the sanctuary, a damning of the holy place.

As the members of the royal house were dressing themselves in foreign garments, so the priests were arming themselves with foreign worship practices.

This seems to be the implication of the phrasing, "who avoid stepping on the threshold." This practice reflects a superstition of the Philistines which developed when the holy ark of Israel was captive in the pagan temple of the supposed god Dagon.

Remember the story? The holy ark was in an unholy place, but the symbol of pagan superstition had fallen before the symbol of the presence of Yahweh. Head and hands of the deposed deity lay smashed upon the threshold of the temple. The priests of this impotent deity dared not step on the threshold from that day forward, like little children afraid to step on the cracks as they make their way along a sidewalk.

Think of it now! Here were priests of the Lord in the right place where his glory was manifest. Yet these Hebrew priests had adopted the practices of pagan priests, superstitious over their broken, crumbling god.

The Lord Yahweh was in the process of finding new quarters. The place he had established for revealing his glory among his people was now an embarrassment to him. He calls it now "the house of *their* lords." The scorn of the Lord is felt in these words. Because of their acts of contamination . . .

He has disowned the house.

He is soon to move.

A vacancy sign is over the ark.

But first, the judgment!

A Taunt from on High

Verses 10-11 present something quite unpleasant, a taunt song from God. This is the lion's roar. This is a call for fright. It is a great deal more than the cackle of the wicked witch of the north. It is the stern announcement by Yahweh that judgment is sure and destruction is soon.

> "On that day," declares Yahweh,
>> "a cry will go up from the Fish Gate,
>> wailing from the New Quarter,
>> and a loud crash from the hills.
> Wail, you who live in the market district;
>> all your merchants will be wiped out,
>> all who trade with silver will be ruined."
>> (Zephaniah 1:10-11 NIV)

By repetition of similar words, these two verses go together as announcement and taunting response. The solemnity of the section is protected by the interjection, "declares Yahweh." These words, translated elsewhere as "solemn utterance of Yahweh," are a grand statement of awe and wonder.

Think of it. God is speaking. But he is not speaking kindly. This word is in wrath.

Various sections of the city of Jerusalem and the surrounding hills will howl together in desolation. Merchants (literally "people of Canaan"—itself a suspicious term!) and money traders come under special judgment because of a break with the demands of Torah. Since the time of Joshua, the surviving people of Canaan who continued to live in the land along with Hebrew settlers affected them for evil. So much did God see of the old people's attitudes and actions among his new people, that the new people had become the old. Hebrews were now "Canaanites" through and through.

Traders in money (literally "weighers of silver") are excoriated not because there was something inherently evil in their trade. Certainly the context suggests it was the manner of their trading. Abuse of people and contamination with paganism became a part of their lifestyle. As in the actions of Jesus in driving the money changers from his Father's house of prayer (Matthew 21:12-13), so the Lord Yahweh is about to destroy these money changers from his courts.

Uncanny, isn't it? The lessons the priests and people were supposed to have learned in the time of Zephaniah reappeared during the days of the life of our Lord. These attitudes and actions reappear continually! Such is the manner of sinful men.

Diogenes's Search

Remember the story of the Greek cynic Diogenes of Sinope? The word "eccentric" may have been developed just for him. He is said to have slept in a tub and walked barefoot, and is identified by trivia buffs as the early Greek philosopher who held up a lantern to strangers at midday saying, "I'm looking for an honest man."

Long before this caustic cynic began his fruitless search for honest men, the prophet Zephaniah described God coming to his city carrying oil lamps looking for wicked men:

> And it will be in that time,
>   I will carefully search out Jerusalem
>   by lamps,
> and I will visit in wrath upon the men
>   who linger over the dregs,
>   and who say in their hearts,
>   "Yahweh does neither good nor evil."
> Their wealth will become plunder,
>   their houses a devastation.
> For they will build houses,
>   but not live in them;
> they will plant vineyards,
>   but will not drink their wine.
>   (Zephaniah 1:12-13)

As one reads this judgmental section there is a tendency of the temperance lecturer to hit hard the fact that these men are drinking wine. This is hardly the point.

It is not what they are drinking; it is their attitude toward God as they linger over their drinks. The issue is that they are like men drinking beer in pubs in our own day who discuss endlessly ("to the dregs") the affairs of the world and who conclude that God will never do anything for good or ill.

It's a scene from a popular, award-winning television program of the mid-1980s. It's right out of *Cheers*. Lingering over the dregs. What a picture of the barroom philosopher. These people have given up on the judgment work of God; but they themselves are about to be judged by him.

They believe that God is dead. Or if God is alive, it hardly matters. They have built their own sources of strength in their possessions and wealth, their houses and vineyards.

But Yahweh is not like an old dog with no good teeth left. He is coming in terrible rage and will turn their sources of power into instruments of their own destruction. Their own houses will become devastation, even as Isaiah prophesied a hundred years earlier (Isaiah 6:11). God reiterates his message of judgment through his new prophet. It is still coming. The trouble to come was unimaginable.

The imagery of building houses and planting vineyards but not enjoying them is not unique to Zephaniah. Much the same language is used by Amos (5:11). It is likely that Zephaniah borrowed this terminology from the earlier prophet, much like preachers still use the great quotes of Spurgeon today. Again, the issue is not that it is wrong to build a house or to plant a vineyard. The point is that the judgment will come before the house is finished or the vines are producing.

Judgment is coming. Admittedly, this is not the message people want today when they think of the future. It's far more entertaining to read spurious accounts of supposed manuscripts that speak of spiritual E.T.'s coming for a visit before the year is out.

Further, the issues of this section of Zephaniah hardly relate to us today. These issues are of ostentatious wealth, pagan practices, defrauding the poor, complacently denying the reality of God in the affairs of man.

No, these things have little to do with us. Let's go hoist a couple at the corner bar. Let's drink deeply, lingering over the dregs. Let's give life some thought. God isn't going to do anything. Perhaps that scroll is right and another will come from outer space to make things right and heal disease.

Or maybe we can talk about a statue that weeps.

"Say—"

PREPARATIONS FOR THE GREAT DAY

"What's that sound?"

"Did you hear anything?"

"Is that someone coming? What's he doing with a lamp?"

---

1. Eugenia Zukerman, "The Power of Music and the Music of Power," *Theology Today*, XL:3 (October 1983), 328-29.

5

The
Great Day

Some things are very pleasant. Just the thought of them warms and moves us. For each of us there are different triggers for such satisfying feelings and emotions. For Jeff Ray, a writer for the Sky West in-flight magazine *Midflight*, there are three things that bring meaning and pleasure to life. In a whimsical piece describing his company's annual retreat on beautiful Lake Powell at the Glen Canyon Dam in Utah, he writes these words:

> It comes to me now that there are really just three things in my life that matter: vacation time at Lake Powell, a chili dog from Pink's in L.A. (corner of Beverly and La Brea), and Linda Evans (a.k.a. *Dynasty's* Krystle Carrington).[1]

You may never have been to Lake Powell, and you may prefer Big Macs to chili dogs, and care not a bit about Linda Evans (although the last would be a sadness!). But doubtless some things in life are especially pleasurable to you.

There are also things that are not pleasurable. We usually try to avoid those things. Who needs extra stress?

Some things simply are not pleasant at all. One of the most unpleasant things in all the Bible is the judgment scene of the coming Great Day of Yahweh. To some it may seem that only a degenerate could take pleasure in the concept of an all-consuming judgment that is inevitable and inescapable.

Yet Scripture was not given merely to please us. Some of the strong stuff of the Bible was given for our warning. For it to work, it must make us uncomfortable. In order that our warning be adequate, the true nature of the judgment needs to be presented. This is the case in announcing the day of the Lord.

A Description of the Day

Here are Zephaniah's words describing that day. His words are the classic expression. Take a deep breath, then read them slowly. This text is a long way from a vacation on Lake Powell thinking of chili dogs and Linda Evans. But the important meaning of this text may not be very far away at all.

> The great day of Yahweh is near—
> near and coming quickly.
> Listen! The cry on the day of Yahweh will be
> bitter,
> the shouting of the warrior there.
> That day will be a day of wrath,
> a day of distress and anguish,
> a day of trouble and ruin,
> a day of darkness and gloom,
> a day of clouds and blackness,
> a day of trumpet and battle cry
> against the fortified cities
> and against the corner towers.
> (Zephaniah 1:14-16 NIV)

In words of unrelieved severity, the prophet records the announcement of Yahweh concerning the impending day of judgment. Several factors about this day need to be observed:

• It is Yahweh's day.

Sometimes we sing the chorus, "This is the day that the Lord has made; / let us rejoice and be glad in

it." These words from Psalm 118:24 are far more profound than we usually realize. They speak in fact of the
coming day of the sacrifice of God's Son Y'shua (as the
words are used contextually in that psalm). Despite
the sobering reality of the death of our Lord that was
soon to come, the salvation he would bring by his
death becomes a reason for singing. The rejected stone
becomes the capstone, the crucified Savior becomes
the risen victor. I have written along these lines in *Lord
of Song*.

The day of the Lord described in Zephaniah is very
different than the glad day of Psalm 118. This is not a
day for rejoicing. It is a day in which the Lord will be
particularly active in the affairs of men, but in over-
whelming judgment.

This day belongs to Yahweh. That it is called the
Day of Yahweh brings significant emphasis to his role
in that day. He is sovereign. He is active. He is near.
He is coming. It is *his* day.

 • It is soon to come.

The Bible regularly presents end-time events as
"soon to come," "near," "coming quickly." The Spirit
of God wishes his people to live in a state of constant
anticipation. The correct biblical stance is to believe
that we live on the edge of the ages, the precipice of
time. Just a step away is the impending reality of the
coming of God's kingdom.

I had a student a few years ago named Jack Buck. I
don't think I shall ever forget a sermon he preached
one day in class. It was entitled "Short Time." Jack had
been in the military and he used an expression he had
learned in that experience. When a person was draw-
ing near the end of his tour of duty, he was said to be
living "on short time." You could tell this was true, he
told us, because there often developed a very careful
attitude about life and duty. A fellow did not want anything, small or great, to interfere with his impending
release.

Jack said that all of us should live our lives as Christians as though we were "on short time." None of us knows how much time we have; to live today as though we have decades ahead of us is a presumption.

Two weeks after his sermon, and a few days after a routine physical exam where he was judged to be in sound health, Jack Buck died in his sleep. He had lived his life as though he were "on short time." It turned out he was; he wasn't ashamed when his time was up.

When the Bible speaks of the impending judgment of God or the imminent return of the Lord Jesus, the teaching point of this language is to impel us to live as though we are "on short time." Zephaniah says that the day of Yahweh is "coming quickly" (1:14).

- It will be terrible.

There is no accounting for the severity of the judgment of God on this impending day. Zephaniah says strong men will scream when the day breaks forth. Panic and terror will seize people on all sides.

There is a darkness to the day that seems to take us back to the original state of chaos as described in the beginning:

> Now the earth was formless and empty,
>   darkness was over the surface of the deep,
> and the Spirit of God was hovering over the
>   waters.
>
> (Genesis 1:2 NIV)

In the primordial scene in Genesis, God is about to bring form to the formlessness, fullness to the emptiness, light to the darkness, and to cause dry land to rise out of the seas. He was going from chaos to cosmos, from an empty formlessness to a gloriously full and wondrously fashioned world, from a watery darkness to an ordered interplay of light and darkness and of night and day.

In the awful and distressing coming day, darkness descends as a shroud, gloom as a blanket. Wrapped in darkness and gloom, the day comes ever nearer.

Zephaniah says of the day,

> a day of darkness and gloom,
> a day of clouds and blackness. (1:15 NIV)

There were precursors of this day of darkness. One came in the experience of Israel in Egypt when the Lord brought upon that land a plague of darkness (Exodus 10:21-23). The supernatural darkness that came upon the Egyptians, but which did not touch the people of Israel, was a terrifying sign of the judgment that was soon to come.

There was also a sense of darkness and pervading doom in the days of Isaiah during the aftermath of the incursions of Tiglath Pileser III into the Levant. In three successive campaigns (734-732 B.C.) the Assyrians brought under their control the eastern coastlands of the Mediterranean, the midlands of Israel, and the region of Transjordan. Isaiah described the peoples of that day as lost and befuddled in the gloom and darkness of their despair:

> Then they will look toward the earth and see
> only distress and darkness and fearful gloom,
> and they will be thrust into utter darkness.
> (Isaiah 8:22 NIV)

But then a day will come, Isaiah assures the faithful, when the gloom and despair of his time would be transformed into light and joy (Isaiah 9:1-7). We understand his words of promise to relate directly to the coming of the promised one, Jesus of Nazareth, whose preaching in Galilee brought the very light Isaiah promised (see Matthew 4:12-17), and whose still future rule on the throne of David will dispel darkness completely.

For these reasons Isaiah was able to write at a later time:

> Arise, shine, for your light has come,
> and the glory of Yahweh rises upon you.

> See, darkness covers the earth
>> and thick darkness is over the peoples,
> But Yahweh rises upon you
>> and his glory appears over you.
> Nations will come to your light,
>> and kings to the brightness of your dawn.
>> (Isaiah 60:1-3 NIV)

Before we experience the blessedness of God's light through the Lord Jesus, we have to face the issue of impending darkness. Unpleasant as this is, we still must try to understand the prophet's words.

The Meaning of the Day

And what is this day? *The day of Yahweh is any period of time in which he is unusually working in the affairs of mankind, either for judgment or for blessing.* God is never uninvolved in the affairs of mankind, of course. But the Bible does speak of his special involvement, his particular and periodic actions in the affairs of mankind. These periods are often initiated by judgment, but will lead to promises of deliverance.

We think of the story of the Fall of our parents in the Garden, and the notice that Yahweh God was "walking in the garden in the cool of the day" (Genesis 3:8 NIV). On that occasion the judgment that came upon our remotest ancestors lingers with us. But so does the promise of a coming victory (Genesis 3:15).

We think of the period introducing the story of the Great Flood, where God is described as taking particular notice of the wickedness of man (Genesis 6:5-7). Here again, emphasis is upon God's judgment. But there is also an act of deliverance for the small family of Noah.

Throughout the Bible the strongest judgmental texts will also provide a window of light, a small door for escape, a notch for hiding, a shelter from the blast.

There is always the promise of the Shadow of Shaddai.

It is particularly the prophets who speak of the

coming day of Yahweh. Isaiah, for example, says that the Lord "has a day in store" (Isaiah 2:12) for the special judgment of the wickedness of man. In that day man's arrogance will be destroyed and Yahweh will be exalted (verse 17). The severity of that day is described by Isaiah in this way:

> Men will flee to caves in the rocks
> and to holes in the ground
> from dread of Yahweh
> and the splendor of his majesty,
> when he rises to shake the earth.
> (Isaiah 2:19 NIV)

These words describe the wicked objects of God's coming judgment who will flee for protection to rocks, holes, caverns and crags—but will not find protection. Those who hide in places other than the Shadow of Shaddai will find their hiding places melting away (Psalm 97:3-5).

The Extent of the Day

And how pervasive is the judgment to come? Brace yourself. Here are the harshest words of all from Zephaniah:

> I will bring distress on the people
> and they will walk like blind men,
> because they have sinned against Yahweh.
> Their blood will be poured out like dust
> and their entrails like filth.
> Neither their silver nor their gold
> will be able to save them
> on the day of Yahweh's wrath.
> In the fire of his jealousy
> the whole world will be consumed,
> for he will make a sudden end
> of all who live in the earth.
> (Zephaniah 1:17-18 NIV)

The emphasis in this text is upon the judgmental aspect of this terrible day. As awful as the judgment is, we need to realize that it is deserved. God is not about to act capriciously. His judgment comes because of man's sin. It has always been so. From the Garden to the Flood, from Egypt to Sinai, from Canaan to Babylon—Yahweh's judgments are based on over-whelming provocation.

When his judgments come they are terrible in-deed. The prophet uses language designed to shock. Think of the value that God places on human life and the symbol of that value which is in the blood. The value of life, symbolized in blood, is so highly regarded by God that he instructed his people not even to con-sume blood in their meat—for "the life is in the blood" (Leviticus 17:11).

But in the devastating picture of the coming ter-rible day, "blood will be poured out like dust" (Zephaniah 1:17). That which God values so highly, he will then devalue. As one might let a handful of dust slip through one's fingers, so the life principle of man will pour to the earth below. In the Hebraic world view, these words would be even more startling than in our own day. The Hebrews had learned from God their own concept of reverence for life. Now God has changed values in a sense, because mankind is in such serious revolt against himself.

The balancing line is more serious yet: "[I will pour out] their entrails like filth" (1:17). The term translated "filth" in the NIV is the word for dung pel-lets. This shocking devaluation of the meaning of hu-manity points out the enormity of sin in the eyes of God. Anyone who has livestock on their place can identify quickly the nuance of this line. As one might shovel out the barn and toss the manure on a compost heap, so the Lord is about to toss with his fork the ref-use of humanity!

Another of God's prophets used similar language in predicting divine judgment on the house of Jeroboam, the first king of the northern kingdom of

Israel. Ahijah, old and blind, received the wife of Jeroboam with direst words of judgment. She had come to ask concerning the welfare of her sick son, Abijah. Ahijah the prophet had no comfort for her. His words were particularly harsh:

> Because of this [Jeroboam's besetting sins of idolatry and religious syncretism], I am going to bring disaster on the house of Jeroboam. I will cut off from Jeroboam every last male in Israel—slave or free. I will burn up the house of Jeroboam as one burns dung, until it is all gone. Dogs will eat those belonging to Jeroboam who die in the city, and the birds of the air will feed on those who die in the country. Yahweh has spoken! (1 Kings 14:10-11 NIV)

In our humanity we grieve for the mother of the sick son who made her way back disconsolate to her home. The prophet told her the boy would be dead as she arrived. Her only solace was that the boy would be buried and mourned, for he was the only one of the whole family in whom God found anything good. But the rest would be destroyed. They would not be buried or mourned any more than one would give special care to dung pellets!

These words of gloom and doom are followed by the shout of the prophetic spirit: "This is the day! What? Yes, even now" (1 Kings 14:14 NIV).

Triggers of the Day

The prophets use current events as launching pads for their prophetic foreview of the events that were soon to come upon the people. One of the most well-known examples is the dreadful locust invasion that came during the life of the prophet Joel. An outbreak of locusts so devastated the land that Joel used that contemporary event as a backdrop to predict the coming future day of the Lord.

The locust plague came in waves, one rushing in

after the other. What the first wave of locusts left, the second ate. What the second left, the third ate. What the third left—which must have been meager indeed!—the fourth wave ate. The vines were destroyed, produce was gone, fields were ruined, even the ground was dried up. From drunks to priests, the nation was in mourning:

> Surely the joy of mankind
> is withered away.
>
> (Joel 1:12 NIV)

These terrors of nature (which Joel understood to be part of the work of God) became the prompting for the prophet Joel to speak of the coming day:

> Alas for that day!
> For the day of Yahweh is near;
> it will come like destruction from Shaddai.
>
> (Joel 1:15 NIV)

When Joel introduces the coming day of Yahweh, he speaks in the same manner as does Zephaniah. He emphasizes the imminence of the day and the severity of the darkness of that time:

> Let all who live in the land tremble,
> for the day of Yahweh is coming.
> It is close at hand—
> a day of darkness and gloom,
> a day of clouds and blackness.
>
> (Joel 2:1-2 NIV)

Joel describes the coming invaders of the land of Judah as locusts writ large (chapter 2). In an almost surrealist manner he speaks of conquering armies as monstrous, mutant locusts. Can there be anything worse than the ravaging of the land by locusts? We haven't experienced anything yet, Joel says:

> Before them [the invading armies] the earth
>   shakes,
>   the sky trembles,
> the sun and moon are darkened,

and the stars no longer shine.
Yahweh thunders
　at the head of his army;
his forces are beyond number,
　　and mighty are those who obey his
　　　command.
The day of Yahweh is great;
　it is dreadful.
Who can endure it?
　　　　　　　　　　(Joel 2:10-11 NIV)

The ravages of nature may be viewed as precursors of the coming wrath of God. When Mount St. Helens, the celebrated volcano of Washington State, erupted a few years ago, some preachers said this event was a demonstration of the wrath of God. I myself liked the Jews for Jesus broadside that suggested the volcano erupted simply because that is what volcanos do. But the fact of the eruption speaks of powers and realities beyond our control.

Every time a river floods, the earth shakes, a tornado strikes, a volcano blows, the thoughtful person reflects: One day all the forces of nature will be unleashed as Yahweh shakes the earth in judgment. These acts of nature are rightly viewed by insurance companies as "acts of God." They are like the locusts of Joel's day. Behind the army of locusts another army is mustering. This is the army of God. They march on a dark day. Soon they come.

The Day in the Near Future

For Joel and for Zephaniah, the immediate outworking of the coming day of judgment was the conquest of Jerusalem in 587/586 B.C. For Zephaniah, this was an event that came in his own lifetime.

Zephaniah was a contemporary of the great prophet Jeremiah. Both were called to the prophetic ministry in the year 627 B.C. Their preaching gave some of the groundwork for the great revival of King Josiah which began in 621 B.C. But the revival came too late and affected too few people in the core of their beings. Despite the good it brought in many lives, the revival was the last gasp of righteousness in a nation romping on to destruction.

When that destruction came at the hand of the Babylonians, it was with unbelievable severity. New researches suggest the city of Jerusalem was under siege for longer than we used to believe. For nearly three years the armies of Nebuchadnezzar surrounded the city, forbidding entry or escape.

The foods were rationed. Water was available, although in limited supply, due to the wisdom of King Hezekiah a century earlier in providing a conduit for spring waters outside the city wall.

But in three years the food finally ran out. The prophetic writer of the book of Kings records this briefly: "By the ninth day of the fourth month the famine in the city had become so severe that there was no food for the people to eat" (2 Kings 25:3).

Jeremiah, the contemporary of Zephaniah, describes these events in much greater detail in his mournful poem in Lamentations. His poem is an artistic requiem for the city of Jerusalem. Lamentations is one of the most highly crafted of all biblical books, the Hebrew poetry developed in a complex acrostic pattern. It seems as though the very crafting of the poem was an outworking of his grief, as a grieving mother might fashion a collage of pictures of her deceased child.

Jeremiah speaks as a participant, a witness, and a survivor of those grotesque days. To listen to the words of Jeremiah is akin to listening to the words of a survivor of Auschwitz. You hear the words as you look from the deadness of the eyes to the tattoo number on the arm, and you sense a living terror.

Jeremiah speaks of the ruining of the temple, whose gold has been looted:

> How the gold has become dim!
> *How* changed the fine gold!
> The stones of the sanctuary are scattered
> at the head of every street.
>   (Lamentations 4:1 NKJV)

Here he thinks of the ruining of the temple, its stones tossed about the city with disregard for the sacredness they once represented. The devastating fires within the temple had caused gold to melt and run between the cracks of the stones. Not a stone was left on another as the conquering soldiers scratched the gold away.

But there is something more valuable than gold:

> How the precious sons of Zion,
>   once worth their weight in gold,
> are now considered as pots of clay,
>   the work of a potter's hands! (4:2 NIV)

As awful as it was to see the stones of the temple tossed about the city streets, worse was to see broken bodies of the men who had tried to defend the city against the relentless waves of conquering armies. Now the bodies of the broken lie about the city streets as so many shards, broken pieces of pottery. Though he had preached against their sinful actions and their stubborn hearts for all his lifetime, nonetheless, Jeremiah weeps to see their bodies tossed about the city so.

Next, Jeremiah takes us to the children. I don't suppose there is any suffering so moving as that of a little child. Jeremiah saw them, knew them, touched them, loved them—and he watched them die:

> Even jackals offer their breasts
>   to nurse their young,
> but my people have become heartless
>   like ostriches in the desert.
> Because of thirst the infant's tongue
>   sticks to the roof of its mouth;

the children beg for bread,
but no one gives it to them. (4:3-4 NIV)

Jackals were notably detestable denizens of the desert. But there is one thing good one may say even about the jackal bitch: she does nurse her young. She is unlike the ostrich who seems quite unconcerned about her young, leaving her chicks to dame fortune for survival.

The loving mothers of Jerusalem were becoming worse than jackals. They were ostrich-like, it seemed. For their breasts were dry and their cupboards bare. Babies had no milk and children no bread. The images of starving children of Ethiopia come to mind—distended bellies, distorted features, diseased bodies, too weak to whimper. So too these little children of Jerusalem were dying in their mothers' arms, and their mothers could do nothing to help them.

Is there any scene more wretched than this?

There is.

It is in the words that follow. Those babies died. And when they died, their grieving mothers, their compassionate and loving mothers, ate their remains! For Jeremiah, this was the last indignity. Far better to have died by the sword than to have died of the famine. The one death is a quick mercy compared to the lingering terror of starvation (4:9). He writes:

With their own hands compassionate women
have cooked their own children,
who have become food
when my people were destroyed.
(4:10 NIV)

The Future of the Day

As unspeakable as the sufferings of Israel were in the destruction of Jerusalem under the forces of Babylon, worse was yet to come. All that has happened in past judgments of God is only a prelude to the future day of the Lord.

It is for these reasons that the Lord Jesus Christ drew upon these very themes when he spoke of the day of the Lord to his own disciples as they walked from the temple and then were sitting on the Mount of Olives. He pointed to the stones of the temple of his own day. With a view to the past and a knowledge of the future, Jesus said, "I tell you the truth, not one stone here will be left on another; every one will be thrown down" (Matthew 24:2). In these words Jesus said the horrors of the destruction of the first temple will be repeated with the second. Then it was Babylon that came to destroy; now it will be Rome. The second temple will fare no better than the first. It too will be torn down completely. This prophecy of Jesus was fulfilled in the Roman destruction of the temple in 70 A.D.

And how does Jesus describe the far and distant day? Well, in much the same manner as the prophets of old. He speaks of labor pains of the coming day. There would be false messiahs, wars and rumors of wars, famines and earthquakes, persecution of the righteous, a falling away of many from the faith, false prophets and wickedness—all these are just the preparations.

When things are at their peak, and the abomination causing desolation is revealed, Jesus says:

> Then let those who are in Judea flee to the mountains. Let no one on the roof of his house go down to take anything out of the house. Let no one in the field go back to get his cloak. How dreadful it will be in those days for pregnant women and nursing mothers! . . . For then there will be great distress, unequaled from the beginning of the world until now—and never to be equaled again. (Matthew 24:16-21)

How touching that our Lord is moved with compassion for mothers of young children during this terrible time. As the prophets before him, so Jesus is particularly grieved for the helpless during times of unrelenting calamity.

The suffering of people in that period of time will be so severe that none would survive if the days were not shortened.

And the accouterments of that day? They are just as the Old Testament prophets described them, with darkness and a heavenly shaking. Jesus quotes the words of Isaiah, which closely resemble the words we have seen in Zephaniah:

> Immediately after the distress of those days
> "the sun will be darkened,
>   and the moon will not give its light;
> the stars will fall from the sky,
>   and the heavenly bodies will be shaken."
>   (Matthew 24:29)

Then the Lord speaks of the sign of his coming in the heavens and the mourning of all the nations of the earth.

You see, it is not just an Old Testament thing, this notion of the coming day of the Lord. Jesus speaks of this day as surely as do the prophets. It is a secure element in the prophetic teaching of the whole of Scripture.

At the same time, the thought of the coming day of the Lord is not pleasant. It is harsh, rough, troubling stuff. Much more pleasant to be on a boat on Lake Powell with visions of chili dogs and Linda Evans dancing in one's head.

But what will come of casual boaters who ignore the realities for too long?

Is it really worth the risk not to think about these things?

---

1. Jeff Ray, "On Three Things Doth Life Rest," *Midflight* (January/February 1986), p. 36

PART THREE

Hearing
the Song

6

Grace
in the
Darkness

It is not pleasant to think of judgment. In fact, the thoughts of judgment we have just looked at are the sort of things that drive some people away from the Old Testament altogether.

Almost unconsciously we may wish to distance ourselves from the Old Testament. For, we believe, the Old Testament is distant from us.

In this chapter we are going to see a surprising shift in the book of Zephaniah from judgment to mercy, from threat to promise. But before we turn to these issues, we should think first about the fundamental issues of the Old Testament in the life of the New Testament believer.

You Must Be Jewish

It is not unusual for someone who spies me studying the Hebrew text of the Bible to make some assumptions. On a plane once, the woman sitting next to me asked, "Is that Hebrew you are reading?" I responded that it was indeed Hebrew, a part of the Bible.

"You're Jewish, then."

"No. Actually my name is English."

"Well, I just saw the Hebrew writing. And then, there is your beard. I thought you might be a rabbi."

I said with a smile, "I have a rabbi friend who assures me that goats also wear beards, but the beard does not make a goat a rabbi."

"Well, if you're not a rabbi, and not even Jewish, why in the world are you studying the Hebrew Bible?"

Why, indeed! Not a bad question. She followed it up with these words:

"Isn't there a New Testament that you could read?"

Why study the Old Testament at all, when it all seems so legal, so restrictive, so binding—and so dark!

Smashing Tables

My beloved professor of Hebrew, Dr. Bruce Waltke, wrote an engaging account of his own change of attitude toward the law code of the Old Testament. In a *Moody Monthly* article he relates how one Christmas his brother-in-law gave him a plate with the Ten Commandments on it. Afterwards, Waltke took the plate outside and smashed it like a latter-day Moses. This was an expression of his conviction that he was not under the law. That law was for Jews in the earlier time. It has nothing to do with Christians today.

Later on, Waltke, now professor of Old Testament at Westminster Seminary, said he came to regret both the action and the attitude that had provoked it. It is one thing to rejoice in the fact that as Christians we are not under the law of Moses. It is quite another thing to smash the plates!

Most of us have concluded that the law of the Old Testament was a bane rather than a blessing. Based on some New Testament passages which seem to speak negatively of the law, our attitudes are negative. The impression most of us have is that the law itself was the curse, but we live under grace. The Jews know the fist of God; only we know his hand.

A verse comes to mind that seems to reinforce this point of view. This is the familiar wording of the opening section of the Gospel of John:

For the law was given through Moses;
grace and truth came through Jesus Christ.
(John 1:17)

It would appear that here we have a definitive biblical statement on the legal, binding, restrictive nature of the older revelation through Moses, as against the free, open, liberating message of grace and truth revealed in the Lord Jesus.

Yet we must step carefully here. Overstep just a bit, and we may quickly slip into an ancient heresy of the church.

Sometimes our view of the nature of the Bible is such that we expect good news in the New Testament and bad news in the Old. Many are simply not prepared to find the idea of the hiding shelter of God in the Hebrew prophets. They are not surprised to find this message in Jesus, but doubt it could be found in the Old Testament.

Marcion and His Friends

One man in the second century of the church felt so strongly that the New Testament was the only source for the good news of God, that he cut the Old Testament completely out of his Bible. He then cut away as well all those portions of the New Testament that seemed too similar to the cast-off Old Testament portions.

What he had left was a very small portion of the Bible.

He went even further. He denied that the God of the Old Testament was the same God as the God and Father of the Lord Jesus Christ. Marcion viewed the god of the Old Testament as evil, the Jews as his enemy, and all associated with this Jewish god as inferior to the revelation of God in the New Testament.

The church condemned Marcion as a heretic. Truly he was.

Yet there are many people in our churches and among our friends who, though they may never have heard of Marcion, are a little like him. It is not likely they have gone as far as he. He really went a long way in his hatred of Israel and the God of Israel.

But they are like him nonetheless whenever they think of the God of the Old Testament as inferior to God as revealed in the New Testament. They are like him whenever they think of the Scriptures of the Old Testament as bad and the Scriptures of the New Testament as good. They are like him whenever they look over at a bearded Baptist in the next seat and assume he must be a Jew.

The eminent John Bright, distinguished professor emeritus of Union Seminary in Richmond, Virginia, terms such people "Neo-Marcionists."

Such people so desire to stress the genuine wonders we know in the Savior Jesus, that they inadvertently malign the revelation of God in the Old Testament.

Grace for Grace

Sometimes Scripture verses are quoted in defense of this approach. Let's look again at John 1:17:

> For the law was given through Moses;
> grace and truth came through Jesus Christ.

It would appear from this verse that John is making a tremendous contrast between the Testaments, a contrast suggesting that *grace* is a New Testament revelation in Christ not known in the law-bound structures of the Old Testament. This conception is strengthened in the King James Version of the Bible which adds the word "*but*" (in italics) between the two members of the verse. These factors might lead one to believe:

- The Old Testament is law, legal, binding.
- The New Testament is grace, free, liberating.

I have recently thought through this verse in a class that I team-teach with Dr. Leonard Hillstrom, professor of Greek at the seminary. I now believe this verse teaches something quite different than we might have thought on our first reading.

Think again what the verse does say. If it is the intention of this verse to contrast the New Testament (grace) with the Old Testament (law), then it must also contrast the New Testament (truth) with the Old Testament (false). For the verse says, "grace *and truth* came through Jesus Christ." If we wish to contrast grace in the New Testament with law in the Old, then we must also contrast truth in the New Testament with falsehood in the Old. None of us wishes to do this. None except Marcion!

I believe the clue to understanding the authentic force of verse 17 of John 1 is in the last phrase of verse 16. The NIV translates this, "we have all received one blessing after another." More literally, the New King James Bible reads verse 16 this way:

> And of His fullness we have all received,
> and *grace for grace* [emphasis added].

The Greek text may be translated, *grace in exchange for grace*. The preposition is *'anti*. This preposition may mean "in exchange for," or "instead of." For example, in Matthew 5:38 we read the familiar words from the Old Testament that limited the action an aggrieved person could take in redressing a wrong: "Eye *for* eye, and tooth *for* tooth." The meaning of the preposition is "in exchange for," or "instead of." That is, you can't go for his head if you have lost only your tooth. Jesus limits retribution altogether.

This preposition may also be used in passages which speak of the death Jesus died *instead of* sinners:[*]

> . . . just as the Son of Man did not come to be
> served, but to serve, and to give his life as a

---

[*] The preposition *'uper* is regularly used in passages relating to salvation as a substitution of one thing for another: Christ died *instead of* sinners (see Romans 5:6, for example).

ransom *for* [in exchange for] many. (Matthew 20:28)

The use of the preposition *'anti* in John 1:16 suggests the way out of our dilemma. It is not that the Old Testament was law (evil) and the New Testament is grace (good). That would be pure Marcionism.

Rather, *there was grace* in the Old Testament; *there is more grace* in the New. God has given grace *in exchange for* grace.

The law was Yahweh's gracious provision to his people to order their lives in covenant relationship with him. The law was good, perfect, beautiful. It is the misuse of the law that is condemned in the New Testament texts we think of so often. The law was given to a saved community to aid them in their walk of faith in relationship to their Suzerain Yahweh. When one began to use the law as a means of achieving salvation, then the liberating force of the law became a binding weight. But the law itself was good, and was given for the good of the people (see Deuteronomy 6:1-3 for emphasis on the positive benefits that come to families who take the law of God seriously).

My understanding of John 1:17, then, is conditioned by the context of the last phrase of verse 16. God had given grace through Moses. Grace and truth have come to be in the Lord Jesus. There *is* a contrast. But it is not a contrast between evil and good; it is a contrast between the good and the better.

In the law of Moses there was grace.

In the person of Jesus there is grace in exchange for grace of old.

He came not to destroy the law and the prophets, but to fill them to the full. Jesus is not in opposition to the prophets and the texts—his whole life and ministry were an explanation and a validation of them.

A Matter of Proportion

So we come back to the issue of the Hebrew Bible in the life of the Christian. The Christian reader should not resist the grace of God that is demonstrated there, no more than the Christian reader should be shocked at the judgmental texts in the New Testament.

One doctrinaire reviewer of a fine book by Samuel Schultz of Wheaton College began his remarks with a categorical negative: "There is no gospel in the Old Testament." Schultz's book was entitled *The Gospel According to Moses*. This reviewer believed the only function of the Old Testament is to show us our need of a Savior, and the New Testament presents who he is.

But this is a one-sided approach to things, a result of coming to the Bible with a set approach, rather than coming to the Bible with questions about its own character.

There is good news in the Hebrew Bible just as there is judgmental material in the New Testament. It is a matter of proportion.

- The Hebrew prophets were ordained as ministers of God's judgment. Their messages are largely condemnatory. But their messages do not lack promises of deliverance and joy for those who respond and repent.
- The New Testament minister is ordained as a minister of God's gospel. This means that his message is largely comforting. But his message must not lack the issues of judgment and death for those who reject and rebel.

The principal difference between the Testaments is not one of kind, *but of proportion*. In both Testaments there is much of the grace of God. In both Testaments there is much of the judgment wrath of God. But they differ in proportion.

When a believer during the Old Testament period listened to the judgmental message of the true prophet, and acted upon it in faith and righteousness, that person was spared God's judgment and was able to find the shelter of Shaddai.

Similarly, when one listens to the offering of the

gospel and then rejects it, that person is accepting judgment because he has rejected God's good news. There is a sense in which we may say that whenever the gospel message is proclaimed, there is also the announcement of God's wrath. For whenever a person rejects God's good news, that person is accepting (by default) God's bad news.

In That Very Day

Now we are ready to go back to Zephaniah to see how these issues of judgment/blessing interplay in his text.

When we direct our thoughts back to Zephaniah, we find the second chapter begins in the very same context as the major burden of chapter one. We are still dealing with the prophecy of the great and terrible Day of Yahweh:

> Gather yourselves together and assemble,
>   O shameful nation,
> before the appointed time arrives,
>   and the day sweeps away like chaff,
> before the glowing rage of Yahweh
>   comes on you,
> before the day of the wrath of Yahweh
>   comes on you
>
>   (Zephaniah 2:1-2)

Here is the same tone.

Here is the same judgment.

Here is the same context.

Here is the same day.

It is important for the reader to see that we are in exactly the same framework we saw in the last verses of chapter one. Only then will the words of the next verse accomplish their astonishing effect:

> Seek Yahweh,
>   all you humble of the land,
>   you who practice his justice.
> Seek righteousness,
> seek humility;

perhaps you will be sheltered
in the day of the wrath of Yahweh.
(Zephaniah 2:3)

I find these words magnificent, lustrous, transcendent.

They are so unexpected. In a passage of unrelieved severity, here come tender words of possible escape. These words are a string of natural pearls displayed on a swath of black velvet. In a text of fierce wrath, here is a gentle sweetness that slips up close and gives us heart. In a context of utter darkness, here is a little light that offers us hope. Here is gospel in the Old Testament. It is even more wonderful for the fact it is so unexpected.

A friend who is heavily committed to producing Bible study materials for groups of lay people told me this story: Bible study leaders announced their group would examine the book of Isaiah for one year. The people were delighted as they thought of the wonderful passages in Isaiah that promise the coming of the Savior.

When the study got under way, their mood changed. The passages of promise seemed few and far between. Too much of the content was judgmental. Some grew discouraged, wondering how long the year would last.

Again, you see, it is the issue of proportion. If we approach the prophets by asking them what they wish to teach (God's judgment on wickedness), rather than just what we think we want to learn (God's promises for the Messiah), then we will be able to enter into their world much more easily.

The prophets were called by God to be his agents of judgment. They called for reform. They preached God's anger. They spoke on behalf of the Suzerain of covenant who announces the covenant is breached and the people are in terrible danger of impending judgment; a part of the sanctions of the original covenant itself.

Think of the beginning of Isaiah. His words express excoriating sarcasm and biting anger:

> Hear, O heavens!
>> Give ear, O earth!
>>> For Yahweh speaks:
> Children I have reared and nurtured,
>> but *they* have rebelled against me!
> Even an ox knows its master,
>> and the donkey the manger of his owner;
> Israel does not even know,
>> my people do not even understand!
>>>> (Isaiah 1:2-3)

The people were in breach of covenant. The judge is at his desk, the defendants are brought near, and the prophet reports the words of accusation that come from the judge himself: They are utterly guilty of an unnatural breach of their privileged relationship with God their father.

The comparison with ox and donkey is odious. Both were proverbially stupid, slow, recalcitrant beasts. But there is one thing even the slowest of creatures knows, and that is where the trough is and who fills it.

We do not have ox or donkey on our little place. But we do have chickens, as I have mentioned. Chickens are rarely celebrated for native intelligence. They may rank with ducks, just a half-step above turkeys. But there is one thing our chickens do know: They know the trough and who fills it. Yet there may be ungrateful, rebellious children in a family who do not know even the barest of things regarding the source of their daily provision.

God's children, the people of Israel, were so witless they were unaware of him and his provision. God says even a donkey would not be that dense. Not even a chicken.

This judgment is so strong, and the words that follow so unrelenting, that we are left quite unprepared for the celebrated offer of grace at the end of the section:

> "Come now, let us reach an adjudication,
>> says Yahweh:
> Though your sins are like scarlet,
>> they shall be as white as snow;
> though they are red as crimson,
>> they shall be like wool.
> If you are willing and obedient,
>> you will eat the best from the land;
> but if you stubbornly rebel,
>> you will be devoured by the sword"
>>> —the mouth of Yahweh has spoken.
>>>> (Isaiah 1:18-20)

This is a passage of exquisite poetry and delicate crafting, marked by word plays ("you will eat" / "you will be devoured") and studied parallelism. It is also the offering of Yahweh's great grace.

The traditional beginning, "Let us reason together," leads one to think that God is offering to negotiate. But this is not a labor/management dispute to be submitted to arbitration. The Hebrew word is a specifically legal term: "to adjudicate," "to reach a legal decision." The decision has already been pronounced: Israel is unalterably guilty. She is in breach of covenant and is now facing the sentence for her rebellion.

But before the sentence, there is the offer of grace. Before the end, a word of hope.

This is the way of the prophets. In the most difficult environments, there come exquisite offerings of God's grace. The people were guilty. Judgment was coming. They could still escape judgment, but only on God's terms.

What we have in Zephaniah is not unique at all. As in Isaiah and Jeremiah and the other prophets, Zephaniah has presented the worst of worlds. In that dreadful setting comes lovely hope. It is just like Isaiah. It is not an unconditional promise. It is an offer that is heavily conditioned on their response.

But it is there!

In fact, it just may be that the relative infrequency of such gracious texts in the Hebrew prophets is the very thing that enhances their power. They catch us off guard each time. And each time, if we think them through, they take our breath away.

The next time I'm on a plane and someone asks me why I'm reading the Hebrew Scriptures, I'm likely to respond, "Why not?"

CHAPTER

7

To the Hiding Place

Let's look more closely at Zephaniah's tender words of comfort presented in the context of the coming day of God's wrath. Here they are again:

> Seek Yahweh,
>   all you humble of the land,
>   you who practice his justice.
> Seek righteousness,
> seek humility;
>   perhaps you will be sheltered
>   in the day of the wrath of Yahweh.
> (Zephaniah 2:3)

As we should expect from a divinely appointed prophet gifted with language and skilled with the use of words, this key passage scintillates with delight in design and depth of meaning.

Let's slow down and look more closely at it.

In the Hebrew text, the words immediately preceding this passage end in this phrase: "the day of the wrath of Yahweh" (2:2). Those words end verse three as well. By this device, we are simply not allowed to think the judgment is past or irrelevant. Judgment is central. The promise of pardon is couched in the pocket of judgment.

The Seeker

Repetition of terms in a brief passage such as this may be a mark of an impoverished vocabulary, or the sign of a skilled poet who uses repetition for emphasis. Decidedly, the latter is the case here!

Zephaniah uses the significant verb "to seek" twice in this verse: "Seek Yahweh" and "Seek righteousness." His use of both objects reinforces the object and emphasizes the involvement of the subject. That is, when one seeks Yahweh, he will seek righteousness, and vice versa. By seeking righteousness, he will vindicate the fact he really is seeking Yahweh. Further, the idea of "doing his justice," is another mark of the sincerity of the seeker-believer.

There is something energetic in the term *seeker*. It speaks of a person who is active and involved in pursuing God. It is not a passive term. Perhaps it is time we revive the term *seeker* to describe a person whose spiritual life is vital and in process. We may have tended to emphasize too much the expression "I found it," leading to a sense of complacency. *Seeker* is more dynamic. It suggests growth and development more than status and standing.

I have anticipated something. It may not be conspicuous to the English reader, but the Hebrew verb translated "to seek" is an overtly religious and deeply spiritual term when used in this type of environment.

The verb bāqaš "to seek," with Yahweh as object, speaks of the deepest level of reality in spiritual things. The prophets build their theology on the teaching of Torah. Here is the basic text from Deuteronomy on the bedrock meaning of the phrase, "to seek the Lord":

> But if from there [the prophetic place of exile due to the people's rebellion] you *seek Yahweh your God*, you will find him if you look for him with all your heart and with all your soul. (Deuteronomy 4:29 NIV)

Rightly to seek Yahweh is an act of faith, of wholehearted devotion, and of deep piety. The expression is an Old Testament equivalent for conversion and sanctification as an ongoing process. When used without a negative qualifier, the expression "to seek Yahweh," means to be rightly related to him.

Another classic text for the positive use of the verb "to seek," is the familiar and beautiful fourth verse of Psalm 27:

> One thing I ask of Yahweh,
>   this is what I *seek:*
> that I may dwell in the house of Yahweh
>   all the days of my life,
> to gaze upon the beauty of Yahweh
>   and to *seek* him in his temple.

Often the wicked are described by the fact they do *not* seek Yahweh. Psalm 14, for example, speaks of God surveying the masses of unredeemed humanity. He is stunned, in the vivid language of the poet, to see that there is none who seek him (verse 2).

Some have objected to the pessimistic thrust of this verse, observing that the world is full of people seeking after God as they look for meaning in their lives. But the psalmist, as the prophet, is using the verb "to seek" in a special, truly biblical sense. It speaks of genuinely worshiping the true God. Hence, when Jesus says, "Seek and you will find" (Luke 11:9), he was not giving a magical carte blanche to those looking for lost buttons. Jesus affirms what Deuteronomy says: *God* may be found by those who seek him rightly.

And there is something even more amazing. Not only may we seek him, but the Father is seeking *us*. In his remarkable interaction with the Samaritan woman, Jesus declared that the Father actively seeks true worshipers (John 4:23). The biblical notion of *seeking* is wondrous; it is the coming together of man and God. It is the serendipity of heaven. It is grace. It is gospel.

The Servant

Zephaniah also places an emphasis on humility. From the teaching of Moses to the teaching of Jesus, there is a leitmotif of judgment on the proud and haughty spirit, an attitude inimicable to authentic biblical faith and behavior.

It is possible to be a proud and haughty person and be genuinely saved, of course. All sorts of rascals are in God's family. Yet *pride* is one of those things that God most regularly condemns in wicked persons. Two of the most celebrated of these passages (Isaiah 14, Ezekiel 28) have been thought to relate not only to excessively proud people, but even to the sin of the evil one himself.

Zephaniah twice uses a Hebrew word for "humility" within this text: once to describe the character of the genuine seeker, and the second to demand perseverance in the walk of humility. He speaks of "all the humble of the earth," and commands them to "seek humility."

One of the marvels of God's grace is the unexpectedness of the relationships he makes. A spiritual pervert might think the Most High God would more naturally relate to the exalted of the earth. As a matter of fact, the reverse is true:

> Though Yahweh is on high, he looks upon
> the lowly,
> but the proud he knows from afar.
> (Psalm 138:6)

Pride is the most pernicious of sins. It is the one sin that has finally won the moment a person feels it is no longer a threat.

Many years ago, the late Dr. Harry Ironside, pastor of the famed Moody Memorial Church in Chicago, was encouraged to do battle with pride. Minister friends who respected his ability in preaching and ministry had a growing concern that he was becoming more and more proud. In an attempt to help him, they made their observation known.

To his credit, Dr. Ironside desired to do something about this all-too-human character flaw. He decided that as the pastor of the magnificent Moody Church, he might do something which would be regarded as unusual for such a prominent pastor.

He had sandwich boards prepared and spent several days walking the streets of Chicago as a street preacher, warning passers-by of the impending judgment of God on unrepentant sinners.

At the end of a week of humiliating and degrading acts of ministry, he came to the conclusion that the "Protestant penance" he had been engaged in had truly done its work. "There is not another minister of a large church in all of Chicago as humble as I," he reflected, "who would spend a week on the sidewalks wearing a sandwich board!"

Ah, pride!

Perhaps the best way to get at pride is by developing the concept of *the servant*. This is one of the splendid emphases of the ministry of Charles Swindoll, especially in his book *Developing Your Serve*. Our family was with the Swindoll family at a conference grounds in California when he was developing that material in a Bible conference. Our daughter Laureen was particularly taken with his preaching on this topic.

One morning I sent Laureen ahead of our family, as we were not finished with breakfast. I wanted her to save a row up front for us in the morning meeting. Finally the rest of us sauntered out in a leisurely manner, confident we did not have to rush for seats with the rest of the people. After all, I was a speaker there also; I shouldn't have to scramble for seats just because someone wished to speak to us at length for breakfast.

We found Laureen not up front, where we expected her, but way toward the back in the open overflow area. I couldn't believe it! I asked her what had happened that she did not get an area for us up front. She said she had tried to save a row, but then another family came along and said it was not really fair for one person to save a whole section of a row when their family had all rushed together to get there on time.

With the words of Dr. Swindoll ringing in her mind, she gave up the row. By that time, nearly everything else had filled in; hence, she was near the back.

Her words were classic:

"Dad, It's not easy being a servant!"

It isn't easy at all. That's why Zephaniah says to people who *are* humble to *seek* humility.

The Shelter

The most subtle element in the words of Zephaniah in this pivotal verse is in the play on the meaning of his own name. He says,

> Perhaps you will be sheltered
>   in the day of the wrath of Yahweh.

Zephaniah's name is built on the Hebrew verb *ṣāpan,* a word meaning "to hide" or "to shelter," plus the divine name "Yahweh." His name means, "Hidden by Yahweh," as we have already learned.

The verb *ṣāpan* is used in a context of confident trust in God, in a psalm that parallels closely our passage. This is the next verse of Psalm 27, following the verse relating to "seeking Yahweh" that we read earlier:

> For in the day of trouble
>   he will *shelter* me in his dwelling;
> he will hide me in the shelter of his tabernacle
>   and set me high upon a rock. (27:5)

When Zephaniah speaks of "being sheltered," he is building on the basic meaning of his name, and pointing to a familiar biblical concept of shelter in the rock, finding the shadow of Shaddai.

The verb Zephaniah uses in 2:3 is the passive form of *sātar,* "to be hidden." This verb is a close synonym

96

to the root of his own name, and in fact is used as a parallel term in the second colon of Psalm 27:5 (above):

> he will *hide* me in the hiding place of his
> tabernacle.

This is an exquisite parallel. Not only does it work wonderfully in this psalm, but it also seals the relationship of the name and the words of Zephaniah in the splendid text of hope, a text of grace in the darkness.

Now that we have looked at the parts, let's come back to the whole. As we come back to this great verse, read it this time with a multi-directional sense. That is, the verse relates first of all to those who heard it from the mouth of Zephaniah as they lived on the lip of disaster. To the very generation that the great threats of extermination came, these words were held out as a means of escape from the terrifying wrath of God.

The verse speaks next to those living amid the continual unfolding of the day of Yahweh. That is, in any period in which God is unusually relating himself to mankind for judgment, these words have a special bearing for those who will read them and heed them.

Notably, these words relate to the time of the second destruction of Jerusalem in 70 A.D. Jesus spoke of that time as well, as we have noted. He also gave his followers warnings concerning the terrors of that day. And he also gave words of hope.

Ultimately, these words relate to the time of the final battle on the earth, which the Bible at times describes as the battle of Armageddon. That is, the ultimate expression of judgment in the day of Yahweh is in the period of the Great Tribulation, and the events leading up to the return of Christ to the earth to establish his kingdom.

Those who are alive at that time, who have come to faith in the Savior, have these words before them for comfort and protection in the time of greatest peril. There will be those whom Yahweh will be pleased to deliver from all assault during that time. They will survive the attacks of the enemy in all its forms. They will be hidden in God's mercy.

We must also explore a contemporary meaning for this text. For we cannot leave this verse for *them* in the past and for *them* in the future. It must speak to us as well in our own day.

Now, in no case is this verse an absolute or a guarantee. It begins with the word "perhaps." I suspect there are two dimensions to this word "perhaps." It relates to man and to God.

The word "perhaps" relates to man in terms of his commitment to the Lord. A minimalist might come along and think that if he or she were to do the least possible to demonstrate a life of trust, then God must be obligated to deliver that person from all harm. But that is not the idea of the text at all. No, these words of comfort are directed toward those who will humble themselves *fully* before the Lord. This is a beacon of hope for the committed, not an escape clause for the half-hearted.

The word "perhaps" relates to God as well. Scripture presents two strongly contrasting truths about God and his relationships with people. On the one hand, God does act in accordance to principle and in conformity with the splendors of his character. There is a sense in which God may be said to be limited in some way by the beauties of his character. Because God is truth, for example, God *cannot* lie. Because God is life, he *cannot* die.

The complementary truth is that Yahweh is *free*. There is a tendency on the part of some Christians, true friends of Scripture, to seize on a verse that is a promise of God, and then to hold onto it like a bulldog seizing someone's pant leg.

There is a point—which only God can measure, I suspect—where this concept of holding God to his promises becomes presumption. One forgets that

Yahweh is *free*. I love the assertion of God's freedom given in Psalm 135:5-6.

> I know that Yahweh is great,
>> that our Lord is greater than all gods.
> Yahweh does whatever pleases him,
>> in the heavens and on the earth,
>> in the seas and all their depths.

One of the marks of the greatness of God, a vindication of his incomparability, is that *He does whatever pleases him.*

That he is altogether good means that we do not need to fear he will act in caprice or on the basis of whim. That he is related to his people by the meaning of his name means that we may count upon him to do right.

But he is still free!

Promises of physical, emotional, and psychological deliverance are conditional, not absolute in the Scriptures. Furthermore, there are numerous ways—not all known to us—whereby God may protect his people. It is comfort enough to know that there is a promise of deliverance. If we are who we ought to be, then we may leave the rest to the pleasure of the Lord. His pleasure is paramount in any event.

The real guarantee comes with the package that covers life beyond the grave. There is no "perhaps" with God's promise of eternal life through Jesus Christ. When we come to the Savior in faith and we receive the new life through our new relationship with him, then there is no small print, no "perhaps."

In the meantime, we assert anew that God is free and he is able to work in the lives of people according to his own pleasure.

For His Pleasure

Let me relate to you a story concerning the pleasure of the Lord. It is a dramatically true account that came to my attention in unusual circumstances.

Some time ago I was driving home from Bellevue, Washington, after a week of meetings. It was late on a Friday night. I had a drive of several hours ahead of me and I was weary. I turned on the radio and began to listen to a talk program as I drove down Interstate 5. After awhile I was about to turn to another station when a new voice, that of a young woman, caught my attention.

Her story began some eight years earlier when she met and fell in love with a fellow who was all she had desired in a man. The story has its rough edges, however; it is a story of our time. The man was married, but in the process of divorce. They decided to live together before the divorce decree was final.

One day the fellow's mother called and fussed at the woman for breaking up the marriage of her son. Actually, the couple had not met until the marriage was already in the divorce process. But as a consequence of her anger, the fellow's mother and the young woman never met.

Weeks passed. The divorce was final. Their wedding date was set. Then the young man died in an automobile accident. Now the young woman was alone—and pregnant. She decided to move back to where her parents lived so she would have family near as her child was born.

The baby, a boy, became the center of her life. As he grew she lavished her love upon him, and through him remembered her warm love for the boy's father. Then her parents died and the woman was again alone in the world—just she and her child.

Then she thought, "I'm really not alone. The boy has a grandmother, even though she does not know about him." So she moved back to the city where she had met her fellow and she got a job at the same place the grandmother worked. They became friends on the job. And then they went to a company picnic where they shared a blanket and a basket and enjoyed the little boy together.

Now she was on the phone asking for advice from a nationally aired radio talk program host. "How am I going to tell her that the darling little boy she made so much over is really her grandson?"

The program host told her that she could not just say, "By the way, that's your grandson." She would have to build up to it and would have to be prepared for rejection. The host suggested that the young woman call the older lady that night and invite her to dinner at her home for one day next week.

"Tell her that this will be the most important dinner of her life. Then, on the day of the dinner, tell her again how important this is. Tell her to be prepared for a shock."

She said, "All right. I'll do it. I'll call her tonight."

Then the host said, "After the dinner, call again so we can know what happened."

At that point I had this sinking feeling I would never know how this story came out. I had been so caught up in the story and its basic humanity that I found it was all I could think about. I turned down the sound and I began to pray for this young woman, for her son and her son's grandmother. I prayed that God would direct the phone call, the meeting, and the reconciliation between these three needy people.

I did not know them. But they were each in need of the gracious action of God. And he is free and he is able to work his pleasure. I prayed that he would bring into their lives a sense of shelter in the shadow of his care.

Sometime later on the drive, I was nearly to the end of the reception area for this Seattle station. I was about to turn to another station when I heard the voice of the young woman again. I couldn't believe it! Programs like this do not let a person call back during the same broadcast. Yet there she was!

I could hardly hear the station now. I began slowing down. I was nearly ready to turn around and head back to Seattle to hear what she had to say.

"You won't believe this," she said. "I called, as you said I should. I told her I wished to invite her to my home for a very important dinner next week. As I said this, she screamed out, 'It was you! It is my grand-son!'"

It turns out that the grandmother was listening to the same program. She had not recognized the voice of the young woman, for she had not any idea that her son might have fathered a child. As she listened to the program she kept thinking two things: "Whoever she calls will be the happiest woman in the world tonight. And I just wish it were I."

And it was she!

The host of the program was stunned. She gasped, "Hallelujah!" Then she was overcome. She went to an unscheduled commercial break. Then, with a voice heavy with emotion, she said, "I don't think anything like this has ever happened on a radio talk program. This is unbelievable!"

And it was.

God had moved.

God had stepped into a situation of hurting people and had done a wonder. I say this, not knowing if any of the principals know the Lord. But I know the Lord, and I know the incident was a work of his grace. This story demanded of me the praise that is due his name.

The next day I asked Beverly out for a lunch date. (I had been gone for a week!) I made the point of our lunch together the telling of this story. As I told her this, she was ruining her salad (by extra moisture!) and we marveled together at what the Lord had done in the lives of those three people. We also prayed that the Lord might use this great providential act to bring them each to a knowledge of himself. Together we praised God. I hope you will, too, as you relate this story to someone else.

The freedom of God to work his pleasure in the lives of people is a constant marvel, calling for our praise. It is also an encouragement that he will work in our lives.

As Zephaniah might say,
Perhaps you will be sheltered as well!

8

And Now the Song

There is considerably more to the little book of Zephaniah than we have room to explore in this modest book. It is not my intention here to present a complete commentary. I wish to open for display some central themes of biblical prophecy as demonstrated in the not-so-minor prophet Zephaniah.

Let's Hear the Music!

For these reasons, I would like now to move rather quickly to the end of the book and pick up the major promises of blessing after the wrath of God has been expended.

Had I my real desire, I would skip the judgment texts altogether. It simply is not a pleasant topic. I've looked again at Pastor Schuller's Bible. He has no highlighting in Zephaniah except for the verse to which I myself wish to rush (3:17). But if that is the only verse we look at in this book, we really would not need the *book* of Zephaniah at all, only the verse. Even the *Reader's Digest Bible* leaves us more of Zephaniah than one verse!

If we are truly to think biblically about the verses of joy and hope, we need first to face quite squarely the verses of pain and judgment. When we do this aright, the verses of joy will mean more, for their meaning will be from the biblical context and not from our own imported, sentimental (and likely unbalanced) views.

It is the way of the prophets to speak of the worst first, and then the best. The prophet Zephaniah presents a text of severest gloom, the outpouring of the wrath of Yahweh. His prophecies relate first to the immediate generation who heard his words, and they were fulfilled in the destruction of the city of Jerusalem in his own lifetime.

But the judgmental prophecies of Zephaniah, along with those of Jeremiah his contemporary, were not exhausted in the events of his own day. The language he uses of the great and terrible coming day of Yahweh points finally to the end of the age and the climactic judgment scenes of the Great Tribulation period and the advent of the Savior to establish his kingdom.

We may survey briefly the transitions in which Zephaniah leads us from his promise of protection on that great day of wrath to his picture of the establishment of God's great kingdom.

Judgment on the Nations
In a manner characteristic of Hebrew prophets, Zephaniah delivers messages of judgment on the nations surrounding his own people. These judgments are based on the particular evils of these peoples. They are listed one after another:

Philistia (2:4-7), judged by God, their lands to become the possession of the people of Judah;

Moab and Ammon (2:8-11), to be destroyed because of their pride in resisting the advances of the people of God on their way to Canaan from the wilderness;

Cush (2:12), to be slain by the sword;

Assyria (2:13-15), Nineveh, a "safe city," will become a ruin, the taunt of passers-by.

Yahweh's intention in judgment is not evil; it is ever good. In the words of judgment on the nations, there is his statement of express purpose, that the survivors to a man turn in true worship to the Lord. It is in the midst of judgment that Zephaniah declares,

> The LORD *will be* awesome to them, for He will reduce to nothing all the gods of the earth; *people* shall worship Him, each one from his place, indeed all the shores of the nations.

The worldwide expectations of the worship of Yahweh, seminal in his promise to father Abram (Genesis 12:3), are reiterated in this splendid text. Judgment, finally, is an act of his mercy, his severe mercy.

Judgment on Jerusalem

The prophets have their bag of tricks. One is to announce God's judgment against the enemy nations round about Judah or Israel. Then when the people are ready to cheer at the thought of the end of their enemies' power, the prophet whirls around and faces the cheering mob. With a long finger pointing right to the heart of each hearer, he proceeds to announce the judgment of God upon his people and his nation.

Zephaniah does this in the beginning of chapter 3. He has spoken with judgment on traditional rivals and enemy states. He has used four directions: west (Philistia), east (Moab and Ammon), south (Cush), and north (Assyria). Each has its day of the wrath of God.

Then Zephaniah turns on Jerusalem. His first word is "Woe!" This is the type of word whose very sound bears its meaning. We call this onomatopoeia. The sound of the word "buzz" has its own meaning. So does the word "woe." In this word there are two emotions expressed: One is a resolute facing of doom; the other is the regret that such has had to come.

By the word "woe" we learn something of God's own heart. While he does what he pleases, he takes no pleasure in inflicting judgment on his people. The prophet Isaiah once described it this way:

> Yahweh will rise up as he did at Mount
> Perazim,
> he will rouse himself as in the Valley of
> Gibeon—
> to do his work, *his strange work*,
> and perform his task, *his alien task*.
>   (Isaiah 28:21 NIV)

Judgment is *not* the principal work of God. It is his alien task, his strange work.

As God turns his righteous wrath against the sins of his people in Jerusalem and Judea, there is a gasp from his heart, a sob of feeling, a solemn sound—he says "Woe!"

Provocations of Divine Wrath

It is certain there must be sufficient reason for God to proceed on a course of judgment against his people. The first chapter has presented his case in brief. Here now is another indictment:

> Woe, befouled and defiled,
>   a city that oppresses.
> She is disobedient,
>   she does not receive correction,
> In Yahweh she does not place her trust,
>   to her God she does not draw near.
>   (Zephaniah 3:1-2)

These words have a sense of outrage that is parental in tone. As a disobedient daughter who has wantonly flouted the values of the family might stand before an aggrieved parent, so Jerusalem is brought before her God. The first words of the verse speak of filth and contamination. They are sexual in connotation. Here is a daughter who has wallowed in promiscuity, and stands now before her father unrepentant, belligerent and unchanged. She has spurned her father's arms, neglected his love, spurned his words. How dissolute this is, and yet how very real.

To speak of Jerusalem as the daughter of God, by the way, is intensely biblical. The imagery comes often. In a later, happier part of this chapter of Zephaniah we will see Jerusalem called "Daughter Zion" and "Daughter Jerusalem" (3:14). Yahweh's son is Jacob. His daughter is Jerusalem. Here Yahweh is a father with a broken heart. The love of his life, his own daughter, has spurned him thoroughly.

Wolves Watching the Hens

To help bring about a change among his erring people, God sent numerous agents of reform. The problem of the sinning city was compounded when these agents of God's reform became new provocateurs of wickedness and aggression:

> Her officials in her midst
> are roaring lions;
> Her judges are wolves,
> who leave nothing until morning.
> Her prophets are insolent,
> faithless men;
> Her priests pollute the holy place,
> they violate Torah.
> (Zephaniah 3:3-4)

This indictment of presumably righteous men has an uncanny contemporary ring to it. How many more times are we going to hear of ministers who have left their wives and children or have ripped off elderly ladies in their confidence schemes? As Hophni and Phinehas served as priests before the Lord, though they really had no regard for him (1 Samuel 2:12), leaders in ancient and modern times far too often become instigators of wickedness rather than modelers of morality.

In strong contrast to the perfidy of the so-called spiritual leaders of his people is the solid righteousness of Yahweh:

> Yahweh is righteous in her midst,
>   he does no perversity;
> Morning after morning he gives his justice,
>   at daybreak he never fails;
> yet the evil doer knows no shame!
>   (Zephaniah 3:5)

This passage is strongly antithetical to the descriptions of the wicked rulers and leaders. Both Yahweh and they are in the midst of the city. But they cannot remain together longer. The perversity of the people finally has driven Yahweh to exercise his wrath.

Yahweh had reminded his people of the judgments he brought on other wicked nations (verse 6). But Jerusalem would not learn from the judgment God brought on others. It was as though they were on an acceleration course, rushing faster and faster in their drive toward self-destruction. Despite all his warnings, the wicked people were still eager to act corruptly.

God had provided for his people a place of shelter. He desired that they find refuge in the shadow of Shaddai, a secret place in the Most High. As high mountain with a lofty cleft, and as mother hen with outstretched wings, Yahweh presented himself again and again as the protective place for his people.

But they would not.

As Jesus was to say of the same city and people centuries later, despite his desire to shelter them with wings outstretched, *they would not.*

Out of the Shelter

Zephaniah builds his theme of the sheltering place in ever delicate subtlety, this time using a new word for the old concept. He states the words of Yahweh:

> I said,
>   "Surely you will fear me,
>   and receive my instruction!"
>   that her hiding place not be cut off. (3:7)

The term I have rendered as "hiding place" is the word $m^{e^c}\bar{o}n\bar{a}h$, from a word meaning "to take shelter."

This word is used to describe the den of lions (Amos 3:4, Job 38:39), or the shelter from storm for other animals (Job 37:8). The word is also used, so touchingly, of Yahweh having his lair in the city of Jerusalem:

> In Judah God is known;
> > his name is great in Israel.
> His tent is in Salem,
> > his *lair* in Zion.
>
> > (Psalm 76:1-2)

I find it so intriguing to see the several ways the prophet Zephaniah interweaves in his book this idea of a hiding place.

At the same time it is awful to realize that God's people no longer wished to be sheltered in his special place, nor wanted him in theirs. Instead they rushed headlong to increase their evil. They magnified their wicked acts.

So now it is time for wrath.

Now it is time for terror.

Now it may be said, *Here comes the judge*!

Universal Judgment

Yahweh's judgment is now announced over all the earth. Judah and all nations are now under the sharp lash of his judgment. Here comes the judge!

> Therefore, wait for me,
> > —solemn utterance of Yahweh!
> > for the day I stand as witness;
> for it is my decision to gather nations,
> > and I will gather kingdoms,
> to pour out upon them my wrath,
> > all the fierceness of my anger;
> for by the fire of my jealous rage
> > will all the earth be consumed.
>
> > (Zephaniah 3:8)

Talk about fire and brimstone! When we hear these words we all begin to perspire!

But then perhaps we try to shake it off. After all, we might argue that this is typical Old Testament stuff.

111

This is not the loving thing we have learned to expect in the New Testament.

But before we go too far down that path, perhaps we should recall the words of Peter who builds directly on the very issues of this chapter. He speaks of the scoffers who deny the promise of the coming of the wrath of God. Then Peter reminds his readers that there was once a great and universal judgment of the earth by water. Next time, fire:

> By these waters also the world of that time was deluged and destroyed. By the same word the present heavens and earth are reserved for fire, being kept for the day of judgment and destruction of ungodly men. (2 Peter 3:6-8)

Then Peter puts the doctrine of judgment in balance. God has not delayed his promise of judgment because he has forgotten. He delays only because of his grace. God is not an ogre, waiting for another victim to fall into his clutches. Rather, "He is patient with you, not wanting anyone to perish, but everyone to come to repentance" (2 Peter 3:9).

We err if we relegate the idea of coming judgment to the "outmoded thinking" of "the more primitive outlook of the Old Testament period." We also err if we regard repentance as something for "them" to do. God's patience and forbearance in withholding his judgment includes his desire for our repentance and our right living. For his goal is not destruction of people, but their perfection. God's desire is not to vaporize mankind, but to make man fit to live in his presence.

And Hell, Also?

To speak of final judgment is like speaking about hell. No one really likes to think or talk about hell. How could one? Karl Barth, the esteemed German theologian, was once asked "Do you believe in hell?"

His retort was considered by his followers to be a master stroke: "No. I believe in Jesus Christ!"

Pretty neat, this change of direction. And it is hard to gainsay one's pledge of faith in Jesus. Yet should not one who believes *in* Jesus Christ also believe *him*? Jesus' words about the reality of coming judgment are even more graphic and pronounced than the words of the prophet Zephaniah. It was Jesus who spoke of dividing sheep from goats, and the everlasting anguish that comes to the wicked who is rejected from the blessings of eternity (Matthew 25:31-46).

Jesus also explained the true nature of eternal punishment. It was really designed for Satan and his cronies; there is a sense that people enter Satan's punishment by default. Jesus once described his own role as the judge of the ages who will say to the wicked: "Depart from me, you who are cursed, into the eternal fire prepared for the devil and his angels" (Matthew 25:41). The doctrine of eternal punishment for the lost in hell is hardly a pleasant topic. But it was an area of major teaching in the life of Jesus Christ.

Kenneth S. Kantzer, senior editor of *Christianity Today*, comments along these lines:

> If Jesus Christ is Lord of our life and thought, then we who are Christians are committed to what he clearly believed and taught. C. S. Lewis put it succinctly: "There is no doctrine which I would more willingly remove from Christianity than this [hell] if it lay in my power. But it has the full support of Scripture and, especially, of our Lord's own words; it has always been held by Christendom; and has the support of reason."[1]

True Worshipers

God's desire among his people is to find true worshipers. This was the stunning revelation of the Lord Jesus when he spoke to the Samaritan woman at Sychar. It is also the revelation of God through his servant Zephaniah. He states this in the context immediately following the terrible judgment of the world:

> For then I will transform among the peoples,
>   pure lips,
> that they may all make proclamation in the
>   name Yahweh,
> and serve him with one accord.
>
> (Zephaniah 3:9)

Some have thought that the "pure lips" of this verse refers to a universal knowledge of Hebrew in the world to come. This is just special pleading from some Hebrew teachers! The issue involves far more than language; the importance lies on purity of the use of language itself.

This verse is in fact a reversal of Babel. Long ago, in the dimmest memory of our race, there was a common language among the descendants of the survivors of the Great Flood. They decided to act in self-preservation rather than to seek protection in the hiding place of God. They used their common language to help them work together in an immense building project, the storied "tower of Babel," a defense platform to escape a flood if God might change his mind about water judgment in a bitter pique.

God foiled their plans by confusing their language. Where they all went to work one day with a common tongue, they all left that afternoon mumbling unintelligibly to one another. It was as though some body snatchers from outer space had spirited off the people, assumed their bodies, but had not learned their language.

The origin of the races and the dissemination of ethnic groups are traced to the confusion of languages at the tower of Babel. As each small group went its own way, they planted the seeds of what became the nations and ethnic groupings of today.

But one day Babel will be reversed. One day all

men and women will speak one language. I suspect there are champions from many ethnic groups who have a good suggestion as to what that language will be!

When I was still a young boy, a dear elderly woman in our Lutheran congregation asked me if I had started to learn Norwegian yet. I was not of a Norwegian family; I didn't know the first thing about learning that language. She said to me, "Ronnie, if you really want to be a pastor some day, you must begin to learn Norwegian! God," she continued, "does understand English. But he much prefers you *pray* in Norwegian!"

The point of the "pure lips" of Zephaniah 3:9 is not that the language will be Hebrew, Greek . . . or Norwegian. The point is that at last people will be able once more to praise and adore Yahweh in one tongue. And, at last, they will be able to work in one accord (literally, "with one shoulder") for *good*. The problem at Babel was that one language facilitated evil; in the coming day, one language will aid in common worship and service to our great God.

And they will come to worship him at his holy hill, the now cleansed city of Jerusalem. They will come from all over the earth, from as far away as people are scattered. When they come it will no longer be to find forgiveness of sin. For sin and pride and selfishness will be history. Those who remain will be the true believers. This is God's message to Jerusalem:

> For I will cause to remain in your midst
> a people who are very humble
> and *who seek refuge* in the name Yahweh.
> (Zephaniah 3:12)

Here we have it again, and again we have it with a different word. The verb the NIV translates as "who trust" is a verb regularly used of one coming to faith in Yahweh in the sense of *seeking refuge* (*under the shadow of his wings*).

The verb *hāsâ* is used in the classic statement of

Psalm 91:4, "and under his wings you may *seek refuge*." Ruth's strong faith in Yahweh was described by Boaz in the same way: "You have come *to seek refuge* under his wings" (Ruth 2:12).

So we have come full-circle in our study. The book of Zephaniah presents in many ways the concept of coming to the shadow of Shaddai, the shelter of the Most High, the hiding place of Yahweh.

Those who come to him will be able to enjoy his presence in peace—the fullness of *shalom*!

And now, at last, the song!

Music, Maestro!

See what I mean about the slogging that we have done? Because we have worked through the dark texts, we are really ready for the happy ones. I should not keep hitting on it (and my editor may strike this!), but what kind of a Bible is it that just gives the "be-happy" verses?

- How will such a Bible prepare one adequately for pain?

- How will such a Bible prepare one rightly for judgment?

- How will such a Bible prepare one even for life?

If there is anything the people of the church need more in our day, it is not less Bible, but more. We need the pleasant verses as well as the distressful. Only with the whole of the word of God may we be able to think rightly about God, ourselves, and the world in which we live. When you come right down to it, *this is the only thinking that is possible*.

Hear now the call for music. As an advertisement has it, "we deserve it." (We don't, but God gives it to us anyway!)

> Sing, O Daughter Zion,
> shout aloud, O Israel!

116

AND NOW THE SONG

Rejoice exultantly with all your heart,
  O Daughter Jerusalem!
Yahweh has removed your judgments;
  he has gotten rid of your enemy.
The King of Israel, Yahweh, is in your midst;
  you never have to fear evil again!
                    (Zephaniah 3:14-15)

This is where history is headed. Here is where God himself is going. God's "strange work," his "alien task" is judgment. *His joy is our joy.* I submit that this approach, based on contextual development, provides more excitement and more enthusiasm for the purpose of God than any other. When we have worked through the pain, then we will really appreciate the joy. This is the way we are. We hardly think of the blessing of health until we are sick. We rarely appreciate the wonders of our bodies until something goes wrong. Unfortunately, married people tend to minimize the joys they ought to share; when disruption comes in such relationships there is usually a sense of loss for what should have been all along.

One who walks through the whole of the book is ready indeed for the music.

Think of it. We are reading words here which the Lord will speak to his people on the other side of judgment. After the great battles, after the coming of the Savior, once he has established himself as King of kings and Lord of lords, then Jesus the compassionate turns to his people and commands them to sing for joy.

Jerusalem and Zion are used interchangeably here for the people of God. Jerusalem is his daughter; the translation "Daughter *of* Jerusalem" misses the mark. It is not that Jerusalem has a daughter; it is *she* who is the daughter. She is the daughter of God as Jacob is his son. These are lovely ways in which the prophets describe God's endearing love for his people.

Did you observe the words I have stressed?

The King of Israel, Yahweh, is in your midst!

Here is the reason for our singing. It is in knowing that he is near. In the coming of the kingdom of Christ on this earth, the most wonderful thing of all will be the personal presence of the Savior Y'shua dwelling in the midst of his people. The prophets delight to speak of this. No prophet says it better than Zephaniah, however. These verses are truly lovely.

His Song

Here it is, now—the loveliest of all. After the prophet reveals the command of God that his people rejoice and sing for joy, then the prophet tells us about another singer—the Lord himself!

> On that day
> > let them say to Jerusalem:
> > > Do not be afraid, O Zion;
> > > let not your hands be feeble.
> > Yahweh your God is in your midst,
> > > a mighty hero who saves!
> > He will take great pleasure in you,
> > he will quiet you with his love,
> > he will rejoice over you with singing!
> > > > (Zephaniah 3:16-17)

These must be among the most exquisite words in language. For those who have a distorted opinion of the contents of the Old Testament, may I say *this too is real Old Testament stuff!* More than that, this is the very stuff of the meaning of life.

How wonderfully these words describe the person of God!

How significantly they speak of his care and concern!

How delicately they broach the boldest of truths: Yahweh of hosts, the eternal one, Creator of the universe, self-sufficient and glorious beyond our capacity to think or recount—*this God takes pleasure in his people!*

Can you imagine such a thing?

After all we have read of his furious wrath, his raging fire, his insatiable zeal for righteousness—here is a text *in the very same book* that presents a truth scarcely to be believed, and yet we dare not doubt it: God wishes to take pleasure in his people!

The people Zephaniah spoke to were Hebrews living in Jerusalem. The first reference in this text is to Israel, God's ancient people, descended from the fathers and mothers of ancient promise and covenant.

But the promise extends beyond them, though still including Jewish people. Abraham was told from the very beginning that God's special blessing on him would ultimately extend to all the families of the earth, for they would find their blessing in his seed (Genesis 12:3). Those who have come to faith in God through the Lord Jesus Christ have come to the blessing that Abraham and Sarah longed for in their wanderings so long ago.

So these words are for us. They are every bit as much for non-Jewish believers, as they are prophetically tied to the future Jewish people who will confess Christ, "and so all Israel shall be saved."

Listen again to these words of grace as we interleave them.

On that day.

These words set the primary context in the coming day of Yahweh. But it is a time past the anger and judgment; it is the time of supernal blessing, when Jesus reigns in fulfillment of biblical promise.

Let them say to Jerusalem.

The first and principal addressees are the people of Israel who are faithful to God, the believing survivors of the day of his wrath. Based on our understanding of the New Testament, we would expect that they are people who have confessed their faith in Y'shua (Jesus), and now enter the kingdom in the coming day.

Do not be afraid, O Zion.

The judgments of the nations have brought great fear on all who have any ability to think at all. But to his dear people, God presents a calming word. They do not need to fear again.

Let not your hands be feeble.

This is a balancing line, breaking the spell of fear. Peoples would have become so traumatized by the judgments of the end times that their hands would hang slack in fear.

Yahweh your God is in your midst.

This is the supreme reality. It develops the idea of God's indwelling presence in the tabernacle and later in the temple. But it goes beyond. Ultimately these words speak of the second coming in glory of the Lord Y'shua to dwell in the midst of his own.

A mighty hero who saves!

What a splendid description for the Savior Jesus! His name Y'shua means "Yahweh saves." He came as Heroic Deity, the phrasing of Isaiah 9:6, traditionally translated "mighty God."

He will take great pleasure in you.

The relatively infrequent verbal root *śôś* describes playful abandon of exuberant joy. It is buttressed by the more common term for joy. Together these words describe "great pleasure."

He will quiet you with his love.

Here is a father holding his child close, giving him strength, and showing his love.

He will rejoice over you with singing!

And here's the song! For years I have been studying the Psalms and have been led by them to encourage the people of God to sing praises to him. Yet here in these words we learn that *he* will sing over his people! This must be one of the most astounding texts in all the word of God.

Here is the song.

He is the singer!

And So We Wait

And so we wait—with such a prospect before us, with such a hope for Israel's future, with such a love of God.

And so we wait, knowing that God will redress all wrongs, heal all wounds, and do all things right (verses 18-19 describe this certainty).

And so we wait, believing that Yahweh is trustworthy who promises repeatedly that *he will do these things:*

> "At that time I will gather you;
>   at that time I will bring you home.
> I will give you honor and praise
>   among all the peoples of the earth
> when I restore your fortunes
>   before your very eyes"
>   —solemn utterance of Yahweh.
>   (Zephaniah 3:20)

And so we wait, knowing the fortunes of Israel will be restored and the praise and honor due that nation will finally be granted among the jealous nations of the world.

And so we wait, as Christians who share in the promises and who long for the fulfillment of all things in God's good time.

And so we wait, even as Yahweh commands: "Therefore wait for me" (Zephaniah 3:8).

And so we wait, knowing that the worst comes before the best; to hurry the time of these events is to rush the destruction of the wicked and to foreshorten their time to repent.

And so we wait.

But we do not wait without hope. Nor do we wait

without thought for the meaning of these words today. This hiding place in the pleasure of the Lord is not just a future reality.

It is *right now!*

---

1. Kenneth S. Kantzer, "Do You Believe in Hell?" *Christianity Today* (21 February 1986), p. 12

EPILOGUE

Finding Your Hiding Place

The principal problem we have in reading a book such as Zephaniah is not really its emphasis on judgment. That is not peculiar to Zephaniah. One who does not wish to think of final judgment will have to pick and choose in any portion of the Bible he or she reads. Underscoring and highlighting will be safe guides for the next reading.

Our principal difficulty, it seems to me, is that so much of the book relates to people *back then* (Hebrew peoples in Jerusalem facing the impending Babylonian invasion), or to people *in the future* (the nations who face final judgment in the period preceding the return of Christ).

Yet the central issues of the book relate to us and to our lives today. Certainly we are in as great a danger of the wrath of God if we continue in the sins of our age as those to whom this book was first directed. And certainly we are in as great a need for the comfort of God as people of any age.

For these reasons, I wish to relate to you a very personal and dramatic story which centers on finding a hiding place in the Savior.

Let me tell you about Timmy Burg, for whom this book is dedicated.

The Story of Timmy

Nearly two years ago Beverly and I were introduced to a family that was hurting deeply. Nancy and Dennis Burg's little boy Timmy had just had his first birthday. Timmy was their first child. They had waited seven years for him. Now he was one. He was also very ill. He had just been diagnosed with leukemia.

Leukemia is a word like melanoma. It is a word of horror. It is particularly awful when it is used of a little child. It is a word that strikes unrelieved terror into parents when the word is used of their own child.

We know. Five years earlier that obscene word had been used to describe the illness of our little girl Rachel. The story of her battle—and survival!—is presented in my booklet, *Praise: The Response to All of Life*. Because of our experience, Beverly and I were invited to draw near to the Burgs during Timmy's illness.

The next two years were quite difficult for the Burg family. Care for Timmy was their constant preoccupation. His needs took precedence over everything else in life. For those two years, care for him was life itself. His disease took him down some dreadful paths. Remissions were interrupted by relapses. The remissions grew shorter, the relapses more incessant. Chemotherapy and blood therapy were the new realities. He went through a bone marrow transplant. As an only child, the donor had to be his father. For that period of time they had to be dislocated to Seattle for a period of four months. The bone marrow took hold. Timmy seemed to be recovering. Some really good days followed.

Soon things changed. He had testicular relapse. We were with Nancy and Dennis when their little boy had to go in for surgery to remove a cancerous testicle. Such a little boy for such a hard time.

Downs now came more often than ups. Soon the wall around his heart was filling with fluids that had to be drained. New radiation and chemotherapy treatments slowed down but did not stop his inevitable decline. During the last few weeks Timmy was very weak and was in constant pain, for which he needed hourly medication round the clock.

Timmy died this week.

As I type these words, it was just a few days ago that he breathed his last. His burial and memorial services were yesterday. The parents asked me to speak at this service. With breaking heart, I thought back over the last two years and prepared my message.

I began by asserting that the death of a child is an absurdity. Any time a parent is predeceased by a child, there is a sense of disorder. This is true even when the child is an adult. Not long ago one of my faculty colleagues at Western Seminary lay in a hospital bed dying at the age of fifty-three. His mother looked to us and said, "It just isn't *natural* for your son to die before you do."

It's especially hard when the child is young. In Timmy's case, he was three weeks short of his third birthday. All the hopes and expectations one has for a child died that day. He never got to go to Sunday school. He never had his first day at school. He never played Little League, never read through the Bible, never had his first date, never got his driver's license. Instead of burying his parents, they had to bury him. They did that yesterday morning in a small hole in a rural graveyard high on a hill overlooking the Columbia River. Less than a dozen people were there at the gravesite. Each must have been taken with thoughts of the foreshortening of Timmy's life. As you think through such a list of things he had never done, the level of sorrow becomes nearly unbearable.

But there is another perspective. This is what I tried to stress to the many friends who gathered later for a memorial service at the church.

Instead of thinking of the life Timmy had not lived, we ought to focus on the life he *had* lived. For no matter how short it was—that life was his life! And that life was a gift of God.

Remember the words of Job on the news of the death of his children?

"Yahweh has given," Job declared. The lives of his children were the gifts of God.

"Yahweh has taken," Job then said. For the deaths of his children were in the care of God as well. God is not the enemy. When he gives life, that is his grace. When he takes life, that is his prerogative.

"Blessed be the name of Yahweh," Job was able to conclude (Job 1:21). Somehow we need to get to that point as we think of a little boy like Timmy.

In Qohelet (the book of Ecclesiastes) we gain a perspective on time from the divine point of view. Qohelet states his thesis:

> There is a time for everything,
>> and a season for every activity under heaven.
>>> (Ecclesiastes 3:1 NIV)

Then Qohelet begins a poem on the times in which many of the activities of our lives take place. The first couplet reads:

> A time to be born and a time to die. (3:2 NIV)

After the poem, Qohelet then asserts two contrary truths:

(1) All that Yahweh does is beautiful in his time;

(2) We may have a great difficulty seeing that beauty, because we do not have the whole perspective. Hence, we have a sense of enigma when it comes to time. Here are his words:

> He has made everything beautiful in its time.
>> He has also set eternity in the hearts of
>> men;

126

yet they cannot fathom what God has done
from beginning to end.
(Ecclesiastes 3:11 NIV)

For Timmy there had been a time to be born.
For Timmy there had been a time to die.
For Timmy these times were in the plan of God,
and they are beautiful to him!

It was not that his life was cut short. It was not that
he had been unable to do so many things we anticipate
a child will do. It was rather this: *Timmy had lived all of
his life*. For him life was a scant three years. For Timmy
decades were months, years weeks, months days. But
that life, brief as it was, was the gift of God.

So we thought back over that life. We recounted
the times when Timmy was well and how much joy he
had brought into the lives of his parents and all who
knew him. We also remembered the times he was ill
and the grace in his face that could respond with a
smile even when he felt really cruddy.

I thought back to one day early on in his illness.
He was at the Doernbecker Hospital, in the room
next-door to where Rachel had been years earlier. The
report his parents received that morning had been unusually grim. Medical signs were all bad. It did not appear that he would live. Death stalked his room that
day.

We wept together, talked together and then sat together. Then Timmy stirred and began to cry. Nancy
went over to his crib and picked him up. Then in that
delicate, dignified way a young mother has, she
brought him up to her body to nurse him, a blanket
draped over the front of her. She sat in the rocking
chair nursing Timmy while Dennis had his arm around
her.

After a few minutes, I asked Nancy a question.
"How do you think Timmy feels right now?"
"You know how he feels! He is in such pain."
"No. I mean, how do you think he feels right now?

"Right *now?*"

"Yes. Right now as you are nursing him."

"Oh. Well, I think he is feeling very good to be held."

"And how do you feel?"

"Well, you *know* how badly we all feel."

"But how do you feel right now? Now as you are nursing him?"

"Oh. I feel really good. This is the one thing I can do for him that really brings him comfort."

A few minutes passed. Nancy began to smile. Then Dennis and I began to smile.

Death stalked that room, and we were all smiling!

I had been studying the book of Zephaniah and had begun to think about the concept of a hiding place—not just in the world to come, but in the terrors of life today.

For a brief moment in that hospital room in a world of pain *we had found a hiding place*. Had you been there, you might have heard the Savior singing.

Yesterday as I related this story in the memorial service, I wondered how it would affect Nancy. From time to time throughout the service she had been crying—as had we all. As I told the story, I saw her smile again, first tentatively, then bright, live and vibrant. And we all thanked God for his gift of Timmy and for the life he had lived fully in such a short period of time.

There is a postscript to this story—its greatest triumph. Timmy's daddy had had a particularly difficult time coming to accept the impending death of his little boy. He so loved him that he despaired of life itself if his son were to die. There were many times we prayed for Dennis that God would bring him encouragement during this terrible trial.

In the weeks before Timmy's death, the little boy suffered so much that Dennis was finally able to come to the resolution that death was preferable to life, for he would not hurt any longer.

Dennis surprised us all on the day of the memorial service. He handed Pastor Don Boldt a small square of paper which he wished me to read during the service. It was a little poem which Dennis had written for his child. Now as poems go, this one will win no prizes. But as feelings go, it wins the *cordon bleu!* Dennis wrote his farewell to his little boy, promising no longer to ask Why, but When, for he knew he would see his little boy again.

And Timmy's death? It was a gentle falling while being held in his mother's arms. His passing was imminent that Tuesday morning, but no one quite saw it come. He was breathing slightly, and then he was not.

He was being held by Nancy, and then he was in the arms of Jesus. Timmy has found his new hiding place, his eternal shelter at last.

I received a note today from a woman who had been at the service. Among her gracious words were these: "I left with tired tear-ducts, but with a *healed* heart."

You see, the central promise of Zephaniah—that there is a hiding place in Yahweh for those who draw near—is not just a promise for those who will face the coming judgment of God in the end times.

Zephaniah's promise of the Shelter of Shaddai can come to pass even in a hospital room where a much loved little boy is dying.

If you draw near to him, you may discover this hiding place in the Savior as well.

No matter where you are!